Jesus Makes the Difference!

Jesus Makes the Difference!

The Gospel in Human Experience

JAMES A. HARNISH

The Upper Room
Nashville, Tennessee

For Marsh

The sum which two married people owe to one another
defies calculation. It is an infinite debt, which can
only be discharged through all eternity.

Johann Wolfgang von Goethe

Contents

Jesus Makes the Difference!

Foreword —————————————————————

The ability to reach up into the theological strato-
sphere to bring down the great propositions of the Christian
faith and then set them to the music of one's own soul is a
rare and precious gift that the good God has reserved for
special witnesses. This is also true of the capacity to put
ancient religious truth into an understandable contemporary idiom. All of this is the more significant when, in such
processes, no damage is done to historic Christian doctrine.

James A. Harnish is blessedly unusual, even in that large
company of committed ministers of the gospel for which
every bishop gives fervent thanks. He is a constantly faithful parish minister whose exciting church commands the
admiration of a grateful annual conference. He is a
thoughtful participant in district and conference activities,
not always presenting predictable party-line positions,
compassionate and constructive in his perspectives. A
member of his Jurisdictional Conference in 1984, his orbit
of concern is now enlarging to embrace world Christianity:
he was a faithful attendant at all sessions of the World
Methodist Conference in Nairobi in the summer of 1986.
He is the kind of balanced and informed evangelical able to
lift that grand old word out of often distressing current
misuse and put it back into its honored historic context.

With it all, he is a genuine and warm human being whom it is a privilege to count as friend.

This is Mr. Harnish's second book. The first was so absorbing that I read it all the way through during most of one long night. In the present volume, he gathers up many of the common issues with which ordinary people wrestle daily, places them under the white incandescence of his own penetrating analysis, and sets forth, in plain but lovely language, the difference that Jesus makes. It is an immensely practical book, sure to be helpful to the average church member, defensible in its theology, and possessed of the high inspiration that good preaching ought always to offer the Christian community.

It is an honor for me to write these introductory words and to commend to the wide readership it surely deserves this splendid work from the heart and pen of a good minister of our Lord Jesus Christ.

EARL G. HUNT, JR.
Bishop, United Methodist Church

Introduction ————————————

THE QUESTION OF A CONGENITAL BELIEVER

Let me introduce myself: I am a believer; in the words of Frederick Buechner, "a congenital believer, a helpless hungerer after the marvelous as solace and adventure and escape." I was born a believer. This belief was native to my being, something I have carried as a part of me as much and as long as my blue eyes, my brown hair, the mole on my left arm, and the twin brother who arrived four minutes behind me.

This is not to say that I have not had or do not still have my times of doubt and questioning, wondering if there is any more to this business of Christian faith than religious tradition and a desire for external support. Nor is it to say that belief has always been easy, any more than learning to walk, ride a bike, or read Shakespeare was easy. It is simply to say that, by a stroke of divine grace, I was born with a tendency toward belief, and, by an equal stroke of grace, I was born into a family that nurtured, encouraged, affirmed, and strengthened that desire to believe.

Put all of this together and it means that I have struggled very little with the question, Is there a God? The serious question for me, at least in recent years, has been, What difference does it really make to believe? If you cut through all the traditional language, all the unquestioned assumptions, all the things religious people tend to say without questioning their meaning, what real, tangible, identifiable difference does the Christian faith make in the lives of men and women during this latter half of the twentieth century? This book is one man's honest attempt to look directly into the face of real-life, contemporary human experience and give a helpful, hopeful, practical answer to that question.

Along the way, I have had a lot of help from my friends. The family of faith at St. Luke's United Methodist Church is one of the most honest, open, fun-loving groups I have ever known. The lives of the members are both the setting for the questions posed in these chapters and the arena in which I see the answers being worked out. I have been blessed with a congregation that keeps me honest and that never allows me to get away with unquestioned assumptions or shallow religious jargon. These chapters have been field-tested in the lives of these men and women who are honestly searching for a relationship with God that makes sense in their minds and a difference in their lives.

On a more personal level, my wife and I have been part of a weekly Bible study and sharing group, a fun-filled, laughter-soaked, spirit-infused circle of friendship in which we constantly ask what the words of the Bible mean when they are lived out in common, ordinary lives like ours. The laughter, love, and honesty of this group have saturated these chapters—so much so, that I hope this book will be a resource for other groups like ours.

Finally, but always first, is my wife. She is also a "congenital believer" (though she may question the expression), a person of simple, honest faith whose relationship with God is never flamboyant but always a source of light for those whom she loves.

Leslie Weatherhead, according to his son and biographer, took it as his self-imposed task "to render the facts of the Christian story in as simple a language as could convey them." He is also described as one who "seemed to love the pagans as much as the pious, perhaps more. . . . His ministry tended through the years to be directed less toward the official Christian, the signed-up, regular member, so to say, and more to people he called 'lovable pagans.' " At this point in my life and ministry, I am attempting to claim this task and this love as my own. My hope is that through these chapters the spirit of Christ will come alive in simple, clear, and practical terms for those who have yet to recognize its presence in our world.

I am writing these words on January 6, the Epiphany of our Lord, the day we celebrate the way God is revealed to us in the child of Bethlehem. I cannot offer these chapters without expressing my deep gratitude for my parents and my foremothers and forefathers in the faith. It was through them that I was first shown the difference Jesus can make. None of the comments in these chapters in any way diminish the debt of gratitude I owe to them for first showing me the way to that child.

To Jo Sattelmeier, my friend and colaborer in the gospel, I offer my word of thanks for hours of typing and retyping without the miraculous aid of a word processor. What a difference that would have made in her life!

Epiphany, 1986
Orlando, Florida

1

UNDER THE INFLUENCE OF JESUS

> Just as acting is more than reading lines, so is
> quarterbacking more than calling plays. The play-
> calling itself is overrated. . . . It is *after* the play
> starts, when he is on the run facing myriad
> alternatives . . . — it is at those most critical
> moments that a quarterback must shine.
> —John Underwood

Read Matthew 11:25-30

The words caught my attention with as much force as would the flashing blue lights and the whining siren of a state trooper on the interstate. They are words of Mother Teresa, that humble saint of Calcutta: "Put yourself completely under the influence of Jesus, so that he may think his thoughts in your mind, do his work through your hands, for you will be all-powerful with him to strengthen you."

The words struck me as a clear definition of what it means to live the Christian life, a very accurate description of what it means to respond to the invitation of Jesus, who said, "Come to me . . . take my yoke and put it on you, and learn from me" (Matt. 11:28-29, TEV). William Barclay paraphrases the next verse, "My yoke fits well."

"Put yourself completely under the influence of Jesus." As I started to roll that sentence around in my brain, I

17

made a number of connections. People sometimes allow other people or cirumstances to influence what they do and who they are. This can sometimes mean that people have surrendered the control of themselves—their minds, sometimes even their bodies—to outside influences that often become self-destructive.

I began to compare this image with that of living under the influence of Jesus Christ. Living under the influence of Jesus is the same as living under other influences in that I surrender the control of my mind, my attitudes, my reflexes, my values, even the control of my body, to the influence of the spirit of Jesus Christ. It is different because other influences can lead toward destruction, but being under the influence of Jesus leads toward wholeness and life.

What does it look like to live life under the influence of Jesus? To put myself into his yoke? To learn of him? The chapters in Matthew that precede Jesus' invitation are like a scrapbook in which Matthew has pasted color snapshots of Jesus and his relationships with people. Let me draw your attention to a few.

The first picture is of a leper. He had been excluded from the community, isolated from relationships, forced to live outside the city wall. Jesus asked him, "What do you want me to do for you?" He said, "I would like to be clean!" Jesus said, "Then be clean." And that day the man returned to everything that had been valuable in his life (8:1-3).

Turn the page and you will find the picture of a Roman officer who had a servant at home who was suffering and in pain. The officer came to Jesus and said, "Jesus, you don't even have to come to my house. I'm a man under authority, just like you. The soldiers under my command do what I tell them to do. You have the authority; just say the word and he'll be made whole." Jesus said, "I've never seen faith like this before! Go home, your servant is whole" (8:5-13). Matthew records that at this moment the healing began.

On another page you will find the picture of the disciples in their boat. Suddenly a storm came up and the disciples were scared to death. I think this must be a picture of how the early church felt when this scrapbook was put together: afraid they were going to sink, fearful they could go under at any time. The disciples woke Jesus and exclaimed, "Jesus, we're going to die!" Jesus asked, "Why are you afraid? Where's your faith?" He calmed the storm on the sea and quieted the turbulence in their souls. In amazement they said, "Even the wind and sea do what he tells them" (8:23-27).

Another page holds the snapshot of an empty tax collector's table by the gate of the city. This is where Matthew used to sit. One day Jesus walked past the tax table and said, "Come, Matthew, follow me." Matthew records that at that moment he got up, left everything behind, and followed him (9:9).

On a new page is a picture of a man dancing in the street, dancing because he was paralyzed, but Jesus said "Rise, pick up your bed, and walk," and he did (9:1-7)!

Toward the end of these chapters is a snapshot many of us would like to hide or say wasn't there. It is a picture of some fluffy, short-legged lambs, surrounded by a pack of sinister, blood-thirsty wolves. Jesus said, "That's just how it is going to be in the world. I am going to send you out like sheep among wolves. The going will get tough, but hang on and we will see it through" (10:16).

Matthew pastes all these pictures into the gospel scrapbook and then puts this caption of Jesus' words across the bottom: "Come to me. Take my yoke upon you and learn of me." This is what it looks like to live under the influence of Jesus. Put yourself into his yoke and it's like stepping into the picture yourself.

Come to him like the leper and he can make you clean

and whole and send you back into restored relationships.
Hear his words of forgiveness and, like the lame man, you
can be set free from the paralysis of your guilt and
learn to dance again.
Exchange your fear for faith and he can calm the storm in
your soul as he calmed the storm on the sea.
Accept his authority like that Roman centurion and he
can meet you at the point of your suffering to bring
wholeness from pain.
Rise up like Matthew to follow him and you will know
what it means to be one of his sheep sent out into a
world full of wolves.

This is what it looks like to live under the influence of
Jesus. But how can I do it? How do I take on his yoke? How
do I begin to learn of him? Let me suggest three ways. First,
learn Christ. We need to know Jesus' story, not secondhand
from the preacher, not off the walls of some Sunday school
classroom years ago where we saw a painting of Jesus,
certainly not from some of the syrupy biblical movies that
came out while I was growing up. We need to learn Christ
by looking into the scrapbook, seeing the pictures for ourselves, and getting the story straight. When was the last
time you looked into the scrapbook? When was the last time
you saw the pictures of Jesus for yourself and knew that you
could step into the story and be a part of the drama?
Second, *think Christ.* In *The Workbook on Spiritual Disci-
plines,* Maxie Dunnam reminds us that we are what we
think. We will become like the things to which we give our
attention. We will become the persons we think we want to
become, and we cannot change that. It is written into our
human nature. Our minds, hearts, and souls are like a
mirror. Whatever we hold in front of the mirror will be
reflected in its depths. If we turn our attention, our think-

ing, the mirror of our minds in the direction of Christ, we begin to experience him in the depth of our being. To live under the influence of Jesus means that we deliberately, consistently, patiently, intelligently think of the words, the life, the work of Christ, and allow him to become alive in us.

Third, *live Christ*. "Take my yoke upon you" calls for active participation. You put on a yoke when you are headed toward the field. Jesus is calling us to put into action in the common, ordinary places of our lives everything that we know of his words and way.

One of the most popular books in the United States at the turn of the century was entitled *In His Steps*. It was the story of a group of Christians who determined that before every decision they made, whether large or small, they would ask, "What would Jesus do?" It is the fascinating story of the effect that choice had on their lives.

There are times when I think such an approach is overly simplistic. There is certainly more to the Christian life than that one question. But there is something exciting, something refreshing, something enticing about folks who simply decide that, in whatever decision they have to make, they are going to begin by asking, "What would Jesus do? Given this set of circumstances, in this time and in this place, what does it mean to live the faith that we affirm?"

The discovery of the real, identifiable, tangible difference that Jesus can make begins with a clear, simple, continuous decision to put our lives completely under his influence, so that he can begin to think his thoughts through our minds, do his work through our hands, and be the all-powerful strength within us.

> Christ be with me,
> Christ within me,
> Christ behind me,
> Christ before me,
> Christ beside me,

Jesus Makes the Difference!

> Christ to win me,
> Christ to comfort and restore me.
> Christ beneath me,
> Christ above me,
> Christ in quiet,
> Christ in danger,
> Christ in hearts
> Of all that love me,
> Christ in mouth of friend and stranger.
> —St. Patrick

2

CONFESSIONS OF A WORKAHOLIC

The enemy of play is taking man "dead seriously."
Man should not do this to himself. Our only hope
lies in the fact that God does not do so.
—Robert Neale

Read Matthew 6:25-31, Ephesians 2:4-10

Every person has to know his or her community of
faith. It is not enough just to ask with the Old Testament
prophet, "Is there any word from the Lord?" Each of us
must go on to ask, "What is the particular word from the
Lord for this particular people, in this particular place, at
this particular time." Each person has to know the home
territory.

I think I know my community of faith very well. I know
myself even better. Some people in this world need to hear a
barn-burning sermon on Jesus' words, "Work for the night
is coming." Some need to hear St. Paul's admonition to
Timothy, "Do your best to win full approval in God's sight,
as a worker who is not ashamed of his work" (2 Tim. 2:15,
TEV). But for the community of which I am a part and for
myself, a sermon like that is about as much help as water to
a drowning person. God's word to our situation is found
more accurately in a question that Matthew records from
the lips of Jesus: "Isn't life more than food? Isn't the body

23

more than raiment? Don't you know that God knows all of your needs before you ask? Why are you so uptight, so anxious? Aren't one day's troubles enough for one day?" (6:31-34).

God's word to us may be words from Paul, "By grace you have been saved" (Eph. 2:5, RSV). We are given value and worth as human beings, not by what we have accomplished, not by what we have achieved, and not by how hard we work. We are saved, we are valued, we are given worth by the sheer, unmitigated grace of God. Paul makes it even more powerful when he writes, "By grace you have been saved through faith" (Eph. 2:8, RSV). Your existence is justified not by what we achieve or what we accomplish but by who we are: children who are loved unconditionally by an extravagant God. Paul discovered what we need to discover: we are saved, made valuable, given worth because we are loved by God; "not because of works," Paul writes, "lest any man should boast" (Eph. 2:9, RSV).

I had an important conversation one day with a very successful businessman. In some ways he was the model of the Protestant work ethic and the postwar business boom: he had grown up in the depression; when he returned from World War II, he started with nothing; by his unrelenting effort, he forged a business that thirty years later was grossing well over a million dollars annually. He had done it the hard way, and he had done it very well. In his fifties, he had open-heart surgery to replace a valve. Less than five years later, they told him that he had terminal cancer. He moved into a severe emotional depression.

I listened to him talk about his work, his life, his faith, about everything that was important to him. I was simply trying to reflect back to him what he was saying to me, allowing him to hear it for himself. At one point in the conversation I said, "What I hear is that outside of your work you have no meaningful identity. You have no real sense of self-worth that is not oriented around your business." He replied, "That's right."

It wasn't long until he died. The cancer killed him, but there was a sense in which the largest part of him died when he realized that he could no longer spend ten to twelve hours a day in his office, that he could no longer be in there pushing and tugging and making decisions and could no longer be the driving force behind that company. When he realized that, it was as if he had no meaningful sense of his own self-worth, his value, in spite of all the good things that surrounded him.

Don't miss this point: this man was a Christian. He was one of the most profoundly committed Christians I have ever known, one of the most loyal laypersons I have ever seen in any local church. There was no question in his mind that he had been saved by grace from his sins. There was no doubt in his mind that God had freely given him the gift of eternal life, and he was ready to claim it. But there was a deep part of his personality into which that word of grace had not been able to sink. He never quite realized that he was saved, made worthy and valuable, not because of what he had accomplished, but simply because he was loved by God.

I knew that man very well. I am his son. Along with all of the good, strong, marvelous things I inherited from my father, I also inherited his addiction. I, too, am a workaholic. My addiction is as real as that of any alcoholic or drug addict who struggles with an addiction to those substances. I struggle with the words of Jesus: "Why are you so anxious and uptight? Don't you know your creator already knows what you need?" I take part in my church of upwardly mobile, career-oriented men and women as one workaholic speaking to others, aware of our common need of a new conversion. We need to know that we are saved and made valuable, that our existence is justified, not by our work but simply because we are loved by God. I have found some practical ways this conversion can happen for us. Let me share them with you.

Conversion always begins with confession. We begin by looking honestly in the mirror and recognizing what we see. We need to acknowledge that we are human; we are finite; we are not God. It's okay to be fallible, imperfect, and human. Did you hear about the rooster who spent his whole life convinced that his crowing brought up the sun? He had a nervous breakdown the morning he woke up with a sore throat. Some of us need to confess who we are and recognize that we are not roosters who awaken the dawn. We are human; the existence of the universe does not depend on us.

Confession moves toward repentance. To repent means to turn around, to go in a new direction. It means to change our minds and our actions. It means bringing the patterns of life into harmony with new discoveries in faith. To repent means changing our patterns if we are to live on the basis of God's grace in our lives.

The third step in the conversion process is to relax, to learn to trust and learn to laugh. That's what this gospel lesson is really all about. Jesus says we don't need to be so uptight, so anxious. All we need to do is seek God's way and will first. After that, all of these other things will fall into place. God lavishly provides for the birds of the air and the flowers of the field. Can't we learn to trust God, too? Can't we learn to relax?

In his book *Confessions of a Workaholic*, Wayne Oates tells the story of a time when he was rushing through the Birmingham airport, sure he was going to be late for the airplane. Racing down the ramp, he passed two men, one of whom asked, "Why are you in such a hurry?" He replied, "I'm going to miss my plane." They said, "You're not going to miss your plane. Take your time." He said, "How do you know?" They told him, "We're the pilots." Every now and then we need to look at our lives and ask, Why am I running so fast? God doesn't seem to be in such a big hurry. Who is going to fly this airplane anyway? The God in whom we place our trust is the God who took a day off. The Sabbath is carved into human history as the permanent witness of the God who is willing to relax. If God can take a day off, so can we.

James Armstrong was once one of the most influential religious leaders in the nation. He was president of the National Council of Churches, bishop of the Indiana Area of the United Methodist Church, an outstanding preacher and author, a persuasive influence on Capitol Hill. Several major religious institutions were apparently dependent upon his leadership. The religious community was shocked when he suddenly resigned from the NCC, resigned from the episcopacy, and broke away from the power and influence he held.

I do not know all of the reasons for his decision, but I do know the impact that decision had on me. I drew two lessons from the story. First, I observed that most of those institutions, which seemed so dependent on him, went right along as if he had never been there. Institutions are like that; they will use the energy and creativity of anyone who is available, but when that person is gone, they find a way to maintain themselves. The point is that from an organizational standpoint, most of us are not as indispensable as we often tend to think.

Second, I was reminded that relationships are primary. Although institutions are not dependent on one individual's presence and influence, there may be persons who are—friends, family members, intimate colleagues in whose life another person's presence makes a difference.

In terms of the conversion process, this story has called me again to confess that I am human. The universe, even the immediate universe that seems to swirl around me, is ultimately not dependent upon me. Repentance means intentionally turning away from subtle spiritual egotism and moving in the direction of realistic humility—the kind of humility Paul described when he wrote, "Do not be conceited or think too highly of yourself; but think your way to a sober estimate based on the measure of faith that God has dealt to . . . you" (Rom. 12:3, NEB).

Repentance also means that people and relationships are primary. Anxiety, stress, and tension block the flow of these relationships. It is only when we learn to relax and to accept ourselves and others that we are able to be whole persons in healthy relationships. In those relationships we can begin to discover that we are accepted, loved, valued, not because of what we accomplish but solely because of who we are as children of God.

As I look at my own life and the community in which I live, I sometimes wonder if the most common, most insidious heresy of our times is our desire to find the meaning of our life, the justification of our existence in the work of our hands. Perhaps the greatest difference Jesus could make in some of our lives would be to lead us to a new conversion, to learn that we are saved, justified, made right by grace. It is not of our work, lest any of us should boast.

> O God our Father, renew our spirits and draw our
> hearts to thyself, that our work may not be to us a
> burden but a delight; and give us such love to thee
> as may sweeten all our obedience. Help us that we
> may serve thee with the cheerfulness and gladness of
> children, delighting ourselves in thee and rejoicing
> in all that is to the honor of thy name; through Jesus
> Christ our Lord. Amen.
>
> —*The Book of Worship*

3

WHEN TRAGEDY STRIKES

It has been about two months since we discovered
that our two-year-old daughter, Lisa, has cancer. Of
course, things aren't back to normal. They never will
be. . . . Our biggest struggle has been to fight
atrophy. Grief stagnates you and the slightest
decision requires monumental effort. Your vision
becomes tunneled and for a while you can see
nothing but your daughter. . . . But God is not
stopped. His will will be accomplished ultimately.
Evil has won for the moment and the pain inflicted
by its victory is not less painful because we know
God can use even it for our good. . . . For now we
will live a day at a time, . . . knowing someday we
will be able to ask God some very hard questions.
—Mike Yaconelli

Read Hebrews 4:14–5:9

The call came as they often come: suddenly, without
warning, out of the blue. On a Wednesday in September, I
ate lunch with a group of men, one of whose wife was
expecting a baby almost any day. Within hours of our
lunch, she went into labor and she and her husband headed
for the hospital. When they got there, the nurse could not
find a heartbeat for the child. The doctor was called in, but
it was too late; the child was stillborn. The tragedy is

29

compounded by the fact that fifteen years earlier the doctors told the couple they could never have children. They adopted two but were elated with the discovery of the pregnancy. It was a surprise, a delightful gift of grace. Across the months they had done everything humanly possible to assure the wife's safety, and it all seemed to be going so well. In fact, the doctors think that if they had discovered the problem an hour earlier they might have saved the baby's life.

You can add your own stories to the list. All of us face them, these inexplicable, irrational, unexpected tragedies of human suffering and pain. All of us ask with the Old Testament prophet, "Why do the righteous suffer?" Why do bad things happen to good people? A Jewish rabbi named Harold Kushner raised that question in the book, *When Bad Things Happen to Good People*, which became an instant best-seller. I want to bypass the why question and simply take the fact of suffering as an operating assumption. Instead of asking why, I want to go to the next step and ask, What difference does it make for me to say I believe in Jesus Christ *when* bad things happen to good people?

I know of no better place to begin searching for an answer to that question than the letter to the Hebrews. Drawing on the Jewish heritage of the intended readers, the writer puts Jesus in the role of the high priest in the temple. Using that picture, the writer makes three bold affirmations about the difference Jesus makes in human suffering. The first affirmation is that Jesus knows "the feeling of our infirmities" (4:15, KJV). Jesus has felt it, experienced it. He is with us in our disappointment, our suffering, our frustration, our pain. We are not alone; the Son of God is there with us.

On a family vacation to Washington, D.C., we visited an exhibit of the works of the French sculptor Rodin in the National Gallery of Art. The centerpiece of the exhibit was *Gate of Hell*. I had not known that *The Thinker*, which all of us have seen copied in cheap pottery shops, comes from this work. It is a massive work; the huge doorway is a writhing mass of suffering humanity. There are hundreds of human figures, twisted and tortured in smoke and destruction. At the top, over the lintel, aloof, separated, isolated from all the rest is *The Thinker*, apparently untouched by the suffering below.

As I gazed up at *The Thinker*, I could not help asking, Is that what Rodin thought of God? I wonder if Rodin was one of those folks who believe God is aloof, apart, untouched by the pain, suffering, filth, and stench of humanity? If so, can you see what a shocking contrast these words from Hebrews are? "We do not have a God who cannot feel our weaknesses. On the contrary, he was tempted in every way that we are." Jesus shares our suffering, our pain, our weakness, our humanity. He feels our weakness; he knows how it feels to pray with loud cries and tears. He is there with us.

Dr. William Sloane Coffin, Jr., is the pastor of Riverside Church in New York and one of my ministerial heroes. His son, Alex, was killed when his car skidded off the highway and into Boston Harbor. In his first sermon after Alex's death, Coffin said he was infuriated by well-intentioned folks who said that it must have been the will of God. "My own consolation," he said, "lies in knowing that it was *not* the will of God that Alex die; that when the waves closed over the sinking car, God's heart was the first of all our hearts to break."

The great difference Jesus makes is that I know I am not alone. He is with me, he is not untouched by my tears. He knows the feeling of my infirmities.

The second affirmation is that "we have confidence to come boldly to God and find grace to help in our time of need." The Good News Bible reads, "find grace to help us just when we need it" (4:16).

31

Looking back over the years, I have no evidence to suggest that faith in Christ will protect us from the risk and danger of a sometimes frightfully painful world. To use the title of one of Kushner's chapters, there are "No Exceptions for Nice People." Jesus never promised to rescue us from the consequences of our own bad choices; the bad choices of other people; dumb luck; or the risk, chance, and danger of the world in which we live. Faith in God is not a Teflon coating to protect us from human pain.

In my experience, however, I have seen the evidence of men and women who have faced disappointments, fears, disease, and death with inner strength, deep peace, and strong confidence that can only be explained by their faith in Christ. They were not released from suffering, but they were given strength and help in their time of need.

Look at Jesus' own experience. When the writer of this letter says that Jesus prayed "with loud cries and tears to God, who could save him from death" (5:7, TEV), what picture comes to your mind? For me, it is that night when Jesus prayed in the Garden of Gethsemane. Luke says that Jesus was in such great anguish that his sweat was like great drops of blood. He cried out, "Father, . . . take this cup of suffering away from me" (Luke 22:42, TEV). But there was no escape, no easy way out. God did not take away Jesus' suffering. But Luke does record, "An angel from heaven appeared to him and strengthened him" (Luke 22:43, TEV). He was not given a way out, but he was given a way through. He could not avoid suffering, but he did find strength.

I thought of that garden prayer when I read an article in which the writer described his son, after going through major surgery, tossing and turning in fitful, drugged sleep. He was thrashing the air with his arms, crying, "Daddy, Daddy, where are you?" And the father wrote, "Where do you suppose his father was? I was holding him in my arms."

And where do you suppose Jesus' Father was while he was praying in the garden? Where do you suppose his Father was when he died on the cross, screaming, "My God, my God, why have you forsaken me?" (Mark 15:34, NIV). We dare to believe that, in the very moments that Jesus felt most cut off, most isolated from God, God was there, tightly holding him. The promise in this belief is that God will be there for us as well. We can have confidence to go boldly to God and to find grace to help us in our hour of need.

The third affirmation of the difference Jesus makes in our suffering is that Jesus can turn pain into perfection, suffering into salvation. "He learned obedience through what he suffered; and being made perfect he became the source of eternal salvation to all who obey him" (5:8, RSV).

Ernest Hemingway once wrote that although the world breaks everyone, some people can become strong at the broken places. Dr. Coffin reflected, "The tragedy of human life is not that we suffer. What is tragic is suffering where nothing is learned, pain that doesn't somehow get converted into strength." The great questions of life are not, Will I suffer? or, How can I escape suffering? The most important question is, Will I use it or waste it?

Martin Gray is a survivor of the Holocaust. In his book, *For Those I Loved,* he tells how he watched his family die in the Warsaw Ghetto and of the almost miraculous way he escaped from a concentration camp. After the war, Gray rebuilt his life in France, became successful, married, and raised a family. Life seemed good. Then one day a forest fire swept across the French countryside and killed his wife and children as it totally destroyed their home and all that was precious to him. Gray was pushed near the breaking point. Some of his friends urged him to demand a legal inquiry into the cause of the fire, to find out who was negligent or at fault. Gray chose instead to put his resources into a movement to protect the forests from future fires. He said that an inquiry would only focus on the past, on his pain and sorrow; he wanted to focus on the future. He chose to allow his suffering to become productive, his loss to count for something. His suffering became a means of salvation.

Isn't that the process St. Paul described in the letter to Rome? "We rejoice in our sufferings, knowing that suffering produces endurance, and endurance produces character, and character produces hope, and hope does not disappoint us, because God's love has been poured into our hearts" (Rom. 5:3-5, RSV).

Suffering can produce endurance. Endurance can produce character. Character can result in hope, but only if we let it, only if we allow our suffering to be turned into salvation by the grace of God in Jesus Christ. It happened for Jesus; it can happen for us.

On a Sunday in September, we gathered in the church; we sang the hymns, affirmed the creed, and laid to rest the perfectly formed though lifeless body of my friends' stillborn child. I neither have or desire simple answers for that kind of suffering. There is no quick fix when such bad things happen to such good people. I only know that the God who saw Jesus Christ, God's only son, laid in a tomb was there. I know that we have a high priest who is touched by the feeling of our sorrow. I know that we can ask with confidence for mercy and grace to help in our time of need. And I believe, though I do not begin to understand how, that in the alchemy of God's grace, even suffering can be turned into salvation, pain can be transformed into hope.

May our prayer, O Christ, awaken all Thy human reminiscences, that we may feel in our hearts the sympathizing Jesus. Thou hast walked this earthy vale and hast not forgotten what it is to be tired, what it is to know aching muscles, as Thou didst work long hours at the carpenter's bench. Thou hast not forgotten what it is to feel the sharp stabs of pain, or hunger or thirst. Thou knowest what it is to be forgotten, to be lonely. Thou dost remember the feel of hot and scalding tears running down Thy cheeks.

O, we thank Thee that Thou wert willing to come to earth and share with us the weaknesses of the flesh, for now we know that Thou dost understand all that we are ever called upon to bear. We know that Thou, Our God, art still able to do more than we ask or expect. So bless us, each one, not according to our deserving, but according to the riches in glory of Christ Jesus, our Lord. Amen.

—Peter Marshall

4

WHAT KIND OF HEALING
DO YOU EXPECT?

Jesu, if still thou art today
    As yesterday the same,
Present to heal, in me display
    The virtue of thy name.
If still thou goest about to do
    Thy needy creatures good,
On me, that I thy praise may show,
    Be all thy wonders showed.
           —Charles Wesley

Read John 5:1-18, 2 Corinthians 12:5-10

The letter was dated August 10, 1984. It came from a friend, a physical therapist, in a distant city and state. This is what she wrote:

I've been thinking a lot about healing for the past few months. This searching began out of a personal need. I'm six months pregnant and have developed a very painful and ugly case of varicose veins that have limited my activity and my enjoyment of this pregnancy. Also, lately in my work I've met several people with physical problems that my efforts have not been able to improve or alleviate: a lady with constant neck and arm pain even after her surgery, a lady with no return of movement in her left arm and leg eight months after a stroke, a lady with crippling rheumatoid arthritis for fifteen years. All of these are problems physi-

37

cians have been unable to correct or improve significantly. They need a miracle, and a question keeps coming to my mind. If Jesus is the same yesterday, today, and forever, if he is the same compassionate loving Lord who walked this earth, healing people of their suffering, why can't we ask for and expect the same miraculous healing in our lives today?

Is there an honest Christian alive who hasn't asked that question? I have asked it as I have stood beside someone in a hospital bed, and I have cried it out when I have lain in that bed as a patient. What difference does Jesus really make when we are sick, when we experience physical pain or suffering? Is God's miraculous power of healing love available in our own time?

This is not a question with a simple, twenty-five-words-or-less answer. I want to take a stab at it, however, as honestly as I know how, by introducing you to two witnesses who can give their own testimony. They have absolutely nothing in common except for their illness, their suffering, and the fact that both of them, in their own way, experienced the healing power of God in Jesus Christ.

The first is the man beside the pool of Bethesda, whose story is told in John 5:1-18. We don't know this man's name; we don't know what happened to him after this event; we know almost nothing about him. All we know is that, for thirty-eight years, he had been sick. We find him waiting beside the pool. Do you remember the hospital scene in *Gone with the Wind?* The camera begins to zoom up out of the streets of Atlanta and, along the railroad tracks and down through the streets of the city, all you see are the masses of bodies of people suffering in pain. That's how I picture this scene. John says there was a multitude of people around those pools. But then he focuses in on this one man who had been there so long.

Jesus asked what the man must have thought were the craziest questions he ever heard. "Would you like to be healed? Do you really want to be whole?" These are good questions. The truth is that there are some folks who prefer the security of known pain to the risk and the responsibility that goes with being a whole person. When Jesus asked, the man said, "I can't get in. Someone else always beats me into the pool." Jesus looked into his face and simply said, "Rise, take up your pallet, and walk." Lo and behold, immediately he was healed; immediately he got up and walked away. When the religious authorities got all uptight because Jesus was breaking the Law to work on the Sabbath, the only defense Jesus would give was, "My Father is working still, and I am working" (v. 17, RSV).

That is witness number one, the man beside the pool at Bethesda. Witness number two is Paul. We know a great deal about him. We know where he came from; we know where he went; we know what he did; most of all, we know he was a man of profound faith. Here was a man who experienced the power of the risen Christ and who shared that power with those he met. He wrote that when he first came among the Corinthian Christians they experienced God's power through "signs and wonders and mighty works" (2 Cor. 12:12, RSV).

Paul had seen it all, but he was also a man with a pain. He described it as his "thorn in the flesh." Ever since the earliest history of the church, people have tried to figure out what this was. One of the oldest explanations is that it was what we would call migraine headaches. Another common explanation is that Paul was probably epileptic and was referring to epileptic seizures. Another theory is that he had trouble with his eyesight. The newest theory I have heard is that Paul was infected with a malarial fever that was very common around the Mediterranean at that time. One of the symptoms of that fever was severe headaches.

Whatever it was, all we know is that Paul described it as a sharp physical pain that would not go away. Finally, just like you and I would, Paul prayed for relief. The verb in the original language is actually much stronger than that. The verb is "to beg." He wrote, "Three times I begged the Lord to rid me of [this pain]" (2 Cor. 12:8, NEB). I would suspect it was a lot more than three times. My experience would be that Paul was saying, "Three times when I had these attacks I begged God, as long as I was feeling that pain, to relieve me of it." Each time Paul prayed, he got the same answer: "My grace is sufficient for you, for my power is made perfect in weakness" (2 Cor. 12:9, RSV). Paul was not made well, but he was made strong. He did not receive physical healing, but he did receive grace. He was not relieved of his pain, but he was made victorious through it.

Now hold those witnesses up against each other: the man of Bethesda and the man named Paul. I would like to believe and I would like to be able to say that the man of Bethesda is the prototype, the example, the model for all of us. I would like to believe that every time we suffer physical pain or illness, the word of the Lord to us is, "Rise, take up your pallet, and walk." I would like to say that the power of Christ always makes everyone whole. But that just is not true. It is just not the case, and it was not the case in the New Testament. What about all those other people around the pool that day? When you hold the Gospel narratives up against the sickness of the day, the truth is that Jesus healed a very small minority of people. We must remember that Paul was not among them. He begged; he pleaded; he drew on all the resources of his faith; and all he got in exchange was, "My grace is sufficient for you."

The statement that the power of Christ always makes everyone whole has not been true in my experience. I have not seen everyone who prays for healing become suddenly, miraculously, physically healed. But I have experienced the voice of the Spirit saying, "My grace is enough." I know people who have not been made well, but who have been made strong. They were not relieved of their pain, but by the miracle of God's love they were victorious through it.

From these two biblical witnesses I have drawn three operating principles for God's healing in our lives.

The first principle is that God's primary intention is always for wholeness. God's perfect will always is for wholeness in our bodies, our minds, our spirits, our relationships, our world. Jesus said to the man at the pool, "Would you like to be made whole? Would you like to become a complete person the way God intended for you to be?" This is the framework in which I understand the healing stories in the New Testament. The Gospel writers did not set out to paint a picture of Jesus as a wild-west medicine man or a first-century television healer. The healing stories are picture windows into the kingdom of God. The Gospel writers are trying to say that if God's kingdom would fully come, if God's will were fully done on earth as it is in heaven, this is what it would look like. This is what God intends for creation. This creation isn't perfect yet, but wholeness is still God's intention for your life and for mine. Some of us receive that wholeness in life and some of us receive it in the miracle of the resurrection, but God's purpose is always the same: wholeness.

Principle number two is a great word of hope. Jesus' only defense to those authorities who questioned him after that healing was, "My Father is still working and I'm working, too." That is the present, active, continuous tense. Whatever is going on in your life, whatever is happening in your mind, your body, your soul, you can know that God is still working and we can be a part of that work in our own time.

I remember the coming of the Salk vaccine for polio. I was young, one of those children who would be protected from the ravages of the disease. I don't remember polio; I never saw it, but my parents did. My parents knew how it felt to live under the fear of polio, and I can remember how happy they were when Dr. Jonas E. Salk discovered the vaccine that would protect their children. Now I have to ask myself, which parent was more excited when Salk made his discovery—my human parents or my heavenly parent? Who do you think it was behind all that? Who do you think gave Salk the desire and the wisdom to make that discovery? Who do you think followed him through the process? I can imagine God shouting for joy, "At last, they've got it!" That is a part of God's divine work, which is always moving to bring wholeness to God's children, to perfect this imperfect world. "My Father is still working and I'm working, too."

Principle number three accepts that space between God's perfect intention and an imperfect world. Until that space is gone, "My grace is sufficient for you; my strength can be perfected in your weakness; my goodness and my grace are yours in whatever you experience and in whatever you face. That will be enough."

I wrote back to my physical therapist friend and soon received another letter from her. Here's what she said in the second letter:

I suspect I was trying to make God into a magical witch doctor. In my defense, I will say this was a new area of prayer for me, and everything I prayed was an honest attempt to be receptive to anything God had for me. But when your prayers aren't answered as you would imagine, where do you go from there? You rely on your belief that God is good. You remember the times past when God eventually answered your prayers in a way better than your own expectation. You rest in God's unfailing love and peace, and when you see a lady crippled with arthritis or a small child retarded from birth or a young man disabled by cerebral aneurysm, you can trust God to work in others' lives as God works in your own. I still believe "the fervent prayer of a righteous man (in reference to myself I prefer to say "a woman struggling to be righteous") availeth much," and I'm still looking to God for miracles or solutions to all of my problems, but it's not with a frantic intensity. I am learning again to wait on God to do things in a better way and a perfect time. . . . God intervenes in all areas of our life, not just the spiritual, but the physical and financial as well—as long as we don't attempt to dictate or instruct but rather wait on God and try to be open to God's directive and blessings.

This woman, like Paul, continues to pray for the healing which she desires; nothing less would be honest. But she also has discovered God's grace and God's goodness to be sufficient for her.

Brian Sternberg could have been an Olympic hero. He set a new world record for the pole vault, but, within a month after that success, he had an accident and was paralyzed from the neck down. While Brian was in the hospital, his uncle came to him and said, "Oh, I wish I could take your place for a week and give you some rest." Brian replied, "You couldn't do it. I know because I couldn't either, if I didn't have to." In an interview for a nationwide magazine, Brian was asked about his faith. What did his faith in God mean to him at this time in his life? He said, "I want to know that my life is being used fully for the glory of God. . . . I do not want my faith in God to be just a result of my desire to get well. . . . Having faith is a necessary step toward one of two things. Being healed is one of them. Peace of mind if healing doesn't come is the other. Either one will suffice."

The man from Bethesda heard Jesus say, "Rise, take up your bed, and walk." The man from Tarsus heard Jesus say, "My grace is sufficient for you; my strength is made perfect in your weakness." Both experienced God's healing in their own way. Either one will suffice.

Come unto Christ
    that he may offer to us
for our sorrow
        an embrace
    our tears
        a cleansing
    our pain
        a balm
    our burden
        a rest
    our bondage
        a yoke
    our joy
        a dance.
    —Raymond J. Council

REGAINING LOST HOPE

In this sudden possession of me by Christ, neither
my senses nor my imagination had any part; I only
felt in the midst of my suffering the presence of a
love, like that which one can read in the smile on a
beloved face.

—Simone Weil

Read Luke 24:13-35

You may not recognize the name of James Gatemouth
Moore; neither did I. He is one of the leading blues singers
in the nation, a recipient of a Grammy award and the W. C.
Handy Blues Award. In a television interview, he was once
asked why his music touches people so deeply. He replied,
"That's easy. Sooner or later, anyone who has any brains
gets the blues."

Depression, the blues, has been called "the common cold
of mental disorders." All of us experience it to one degree or
another, all the way from the "Monday morning blues,"
normally cured by the awareness that Friday night is on the
way, to severe emotional depression requiring psychiatric
care. Sooner or later, "anyone who has any brains gets the
blues."

The word *depression* originally described a sunken place, a
low place in the road. That's still an accurate description.

When we are depressed, we are walking, at least temporarily, in a sunken place, through dark shadows where the visibility is poor, the going is hard, and there seems to be no joy at all. That is the kind of shadowy path two of Jesus' disciples were walking on the way to Emmaus. Commentators nearly always point out that they were headed west at sunset, going toward a night that was falling, until Jesus turned them around to face a dawn that was breaking. Perhaps by walking along that same road, we will discover how Jesus helped them find hope again.

The movement from despair to hope begins when Luke records: "Jesus himself drew near and walked along with them; they saw him, but somehow did not recognize him" (24:15-16, TEV). There is good news and bad news there: the good news is that Jesus walks this lonesome valley with us; the bad news is that most of the time we don't recognize him, either.

There was a little boy whose mother was a nurse and whose father was a preacher. When they sat down to dinner, the mother always asked if the boy had washed the germs off his hands, and the father always asked him to thank Jesus for the food. One evening the little guy had had enough and said, "All I ever hear around here is germs and Jesus, and I can't see either one of them!"

Why these disciples didn't recognize Jesus is irrelevant; most of the time we don't recognize him either. When we face depression, when we get the blues, we feel like the writer of the Twenty-second Psalm, who asked, "My God, why have you forsaken me?" (v. 1, NIV). But the very next psalm, the twenty-third, dares to affirm, "Though I walk through the valley of the shadow of death, I fear no evil; for thou art with me" (v. 4, RSV). When we walk through the valley of the shadow, we feel cut off, isolated, alone. But the movement toward healing begins when we dare to affirm what we cannot feel—that the One who drew alongside these disciples on the road to Emmaus also walks with us.

Luke records that Jesus asked these men what they were discussing. He listened as they poured out their sorrow and their loss. They told the story of Jesus' life, death, and now of the confusion over the empty tomb. They climaxed it in one of the most painful sentences anywhere in scripture: "We had hoped that he was the one" (24:21, RSV). *We had hoped* is past perfect tense, describing an action that was completed in the past. We had hopes, but now they are gone, shattered, evaporated into thin air.

There you have a textbook definition of depression. Almost every form of depression involves a sense of loss, usually a loss of self-esteem, resulting in a sense of hopelessness. Healing begins when we are able to tell the story, to define it for ourselves, to name the darkness and to acknowledge the loss. From a clinical standpoint, Jesus was absolutely correct when he said, "Blessed are those who mourn, for they shall be comforted" (Matt. 5:4, RSV). Only those who tell their story, who mourn their loss, who identify the darkness have any hope of being comforted, strengthened, made whole.

Jesus listened to their story, and then, Luke says, he "explained to them what was said about himself in all Scriptures, beginning with the books of Moses and the writings of all the prophets" (24:27, TEV). Jesus retells the story in a new perspective. He lifts their own story out of the shadows and helps them see it in the light of the long history of the people of faith.

I learned a long time ago that it is not enough just to listen to a person who is depressed. If all you do is listen, you can reinforce the despair, driving the person deeper into the shadows. Having heard the story, it is important to lift it out, to look at it in a new perspective, to see it in the light of hope.

In his book, *Finding Hope Again*, Roy Fairchild tells the story of a friend who visited a woman who had become dejected after a long illness. She had begun to withdraw from her friends and was filled with negative feelings about her life.

> "I really haven't done anything worthwhile with my life," she said sadly. After listening carefully and responsively to the woman, my friend asked her if she could remember a time when she really liked herself, when she felt useful and effective and felt life flowing strongly. At first, in her depression, she seemed not to hear the question. Then, after silent reflection, she began to light up and tell the story of her work with adult education in another community and what a difference this made to the elderly in the community. Soon she rose on her pillow, face aglow. Later, she began to phone friends, letting them know she was still in the land of the living, still worried, but really hopeful about her future and what she could do, sick or well.

Jesus did something like that for these dejected disciples. He helped them see their loss in the light of the past victories. Drawing on that memory, he enlivened their imagination for the future.

It was a seven-mile hike to Emmaus, and the two disciples had to make the whole journey before Jesus revealed himself. Some things take time. You can't rush the process. There is no instant cure. The only way out is the way through. Luke writes, "As they came near the village to which they were going, Jesus acted as if he were going farther; but they held him back, saying 'Stay with us; the day is almost over and it is getting dark' " (24:28-29, TEV). Jesus did. He came into the house, sat down to dinner, and did the most ordinary thing in the world. He picked up the bread, blessed it, broke it, and gave it to them. But in that common act, "their eyes were opened and they recognized him" (24:31, TEV). He did a common thing in an uncommon way, and that ordinary act became an extraordinary means of grace. Jesus gives us eyes to see new possibilities in old circumstances, and that is called hope.

Hope is not some far off, pie-in-the-sky-by-and-by thing with feathers. Hope is the ability to imagine life in another way. Hope is sensing that things could be different. Hope is believing that I do not have to live under the cloud; I do not have to walk in the dark. My loss can be made whole; my hurt can be healed; my self-esteem can be restored. It is possible for me to live and love and dance again. I heard it once in the voice of a woman who said, "I'm beginning to feel that one of these days I'll be happy again." That's hope!

A preacher in Florida went through a severe emotional depression midway in his ministerial career. He said that everything in life had turned to gray, that there was no longer any color in anything. The depression became so severe that he was hospitalized. He said he can remember the day he looked out the hospital window and became aware of some red hibiscus coming into bloom. For the first time in months, he realized that there was something in the world that was not gray. He said he focused on it; studied it; in a sense, soaked the color out of that bloom into himself. From there, he turned to the other flowers around the window and began to pick out the different shades of red, pink, and white. He said that the beginning of his recovery was the day he saw color in something else and began to believe that color would return to his life as well.

What could be more common in Florida than hibiscus? There was nothing unusual about that. But for him, on that day, that common flower became an uncommon means of grace. It helped him see the possibility of new life.

Luke concludes this story by saying, "They got up at once and went back to Jerusalem" (24:33, TEV). There was no sitting around, no taking time to pack, no waiting until tomorrow. They got up right away; they took action; they made a conscious choice to move back into life. One of the tricks depression plays on us is that it causes us to pull away, to draw into ourselves, to go off into a dark corner alone when the fact is that our healing will in large measure depend on our choice to move back into our world, to find new relationships, to listen to other stories, to step into the flow of life.

I remember a woman who showed up at church for worship the first Sunday after her husband was buried. I was surprised, though I should not have been, to see her coming up the steps. I gave her a hug and said, "I didn't expect to see you this morning." She said, "Why not? Where else could I go? I need to be here more than ever before."

I've seen it both ways. I've seen people isolate them-selves, and I've seen people choose to move back into life. I have become convinced that we never get through depres-sion on our own. We only find hope in relationship with others. "They got up at once and went back to Jerusalem, where they found the eleven disciples gathered together with the others" (24:33, TEV). There, in the fellowship of those disciples, they found hope again.

Sooner or later, "anybody who has any brains gets the blues." When we do, the same Jesus who walked the shad-owy road to Emmaus will walk the valley with us. The same Jesus who listened to the disciples' sorrow will listen to us as we name our darkness. The same risen Christ who helped them see their story in a new perspective will help us see our story in the light of faith. The same Christ who gave them grace to imagine new possibilities will give us hope as well. And the same fellowship that waited in Jerusalem for them waits for us to come home.

Jesu, in whom the weary find
  Their late, but permanent repose,

Physician of the sin-sick mind,
    Relieve my wants, assuage my woes;
And let my soul on thee be cast,
Till life's fierce tyranny be past.
· ·

Fill with inviolable peace,
    'Stablish and keep my settled heart;
In thee may all my wanderings cease,
    From thee no more may I depart;
Thy utmost goodness called to prove,
Loved with an everlasting love!
                            —Charles Wesley

6

THE CREATIVE FORCE IN FEAR

[The terrors] were buried beneath the impossible
language of the time, lived underground where
nearly all of the time's true feeling spitefully and
incessantly fermented. Precisely, therefore, to the
extent that they were inexpressible, were these
terrors mighty; precisely because they lived in the
dark were their shapes obscene.

        —James Baldwin

Read Luke 12:4-34

All of us are afraid of something. The first dictionary I
checked listed thirty-eight different phobias; another had
seventy-five, all the way from acrophobia, the fear of high
places, to zoophobia, the fear of animals. Do you know what
chionophobia is? This is fear of snow. There is even pho-
bophobia, the fear of fear itself. These phobias are part of
being human. All of us experience fear. Most of the time we
think of fear as an enemy, something to overcome. And
there is truth in this. Although I have never counted them
myself, I have been told that there are 365 verses in the
Bible that say, "Fear not," one for every day of the year. Did
you ever realize that the first words spoken to the shepherds
of Bethlehem about Jesus are the angel's words, "Fear not:
for, behold, I bring you good tidings of great joy" (Luke

2:10, KJV) and that among the last words of the risen Christ to his disciples are, "Do not be afraid" (Matt. 28:10, TEV)? From first to last, Jesus comes to set us free from fear.

But there is another side to fear. In the Book of Proverbs it is written, "The fear of the Lord is the beginning of knowledge" (1:7, RSV). Jeremiah the prophet heard God say, "I will put my fear in their hearts, that they shall not depart from me" (Jer. 32:40, KJV). The purpose of faith is not necessarily to get rid of all fear. Can you imagine how disastrous it would be if the rabbit lost all fear of the fox? Rather, the purpose of faith is to teach us what to fear and how to channel that energy into creative and purposeful action.

One principle I have learned is that fear can help us sort out our priorities and remind us of what is important in life. Luke records Jesus' parable of a rich farmer whose land bore a bumper crop. Jesus says:

> He began to think to himself, "I don't have a place to keep all my crops. What can I do? This is what I will do," he told himself; "I will tear down my barns and build bigger ones, where I will store the grain and all my other goods. Then I will say to myself, Lucky man! You have all the good things you need for many years. Take life easy, eat, drink, and enjoy yourself!" But God said to him, "You fool! This very night you will have to give up your life; then who will get all these things you have kept for yourself?"
>
> —12:17-20, TEV

Jesus summarizes the meaning of the parable in verse 15: "A person's true life is not made up of the things he owns, no matter how rich he may be" (TEV).

In my life, I have generally been among "rich farmers," folks like this man whose barns and houses are full. We don't have everything we want, but we certainly have everything we need. I thought back across the faces of some of those persons and remembered hours that I sat with them when fear suddenly pounded at the door, when they were shattered by a death, a brush with a heart attack, the loss of a child, a fire that destroyed their home, a tragic defeat in their lives. I could hear the voices of those people saying to me over and over again, "You know, we took life so for granted. We were so comfortable. We didn't realize how important our family and friends were to us until this happened. All those material things don't seem so important compared to our life, our health, our family, our friends."

It is absolutely amazing to see the way the fear of death, the fear of loss, the fear of defeat, the fear of pain can help us sort out what is important from what is trivial. Jesus tells this parable for people like us who, in an infinite variety of ways, hear a voice saying, "Your life could be demanded of you. You could lose all this. Then what would it all amount to?" Jesus says, "A man's life does not primarily consist in all of his goods, regardless of how much he has." "Life," he also says, "is much more important than food, and the body much more important than clothes" (Luke 12:23, TEV). Sometimes it is only a healthy, responsible fear that helps us discover the things that are the most important in our lives.

Another principle builds upon this thought. Sometimes a healthy fear can lead us into a deeper faith. Jesus puts it rather bluntly, "Don't be afraid of those who only destroy the body. Be afraid of God, who not only can destroy your body but has the authority to throw you into hell" (Luke 12:4-5). Don't stop reading there. Immediately, as if to silence any temptation to think of God as a bloodthirsty, vindictive judge leering out over the parapets of heaven, ready to grab some wayward sinner to dangle over the fires of hell, Jesus asks, "Can you buy five sparrows for two pennies?" His listeners can. At this time, sparrows are the least expensive sacrifice available in the Temple. If you pay one penny you get two, but if you pay two pennies you get five. That's how cheap they are. Jesus says, "Aren't five sparrows sold for two pennies? Yet not one sparrow is forgotten by God. Even the hairs of your head have all been counted" (12:6-7, TEV).

As a child, I took that verse literally and was fascinated when I looked around the church in which I grew up. I thought, "Gee, God has a tougher job counting some heads than others!" It is exaggeration. It doesn't matter how many hairs you have on your head. The point is that this is just how intimately God cares about you. "You are worth much more than many sparrows, don't be afraid."

In this context Luke records those familiar words that Matthew places in the Sermon on the Mount: "Consider the ravens: . . . God feeds them. . . . Consider the lilies, how they grow; . . . even Solomon in all his glory was not arrayed like one of these. . . . How much more will [God] clothe you, O men of little faith" (12:24, 27-28, RSV). Sometimes a responsible, healthy fear can move us to deeper faith in the goodness of God.

I have never been one of those people who placed much confidence in "foxhole religion," responses to God that are rooted largely in fear and the desire for self-preservation. Given the alternatives, I would much rather love people than scare them. And yet, when you take an honest look at the weakness of our own lives, the frailty of our human condition; when you face up to humanity's insane propensity toward self-destruction; when you observe the almost infinite variety of ways we devise to brutalize, hurt, and injure each other, you soon come to the conclusion that there is nothing wrong with a strong, healthy fear of the things that simmer just underneath the thin crust of our sophisticated veneer. An honest fear can lead us in the direction of a deeper faith in the God who counts the hairs on our heads, who loves us with an infinite love.

As I think back across the lives of men and women with

whom I have shared times of fear, I discover several responses to the reality of that fear. Some of these people were shattered by it, like crystal thrown down on a terrazzo floor; their lives were splintered and broken. Some became hard and cold, building a concrete wall around their feelings and their emotions, totally unable to share their vulnerability, their insecurity, their fear with anyone else, even the people closest to them. Some grabbed for a religious witch doctor who could give them an instant trinket, a magic potion that would take all their problems away and make life rosy again. But there are others who, when confronted with the reality of fear, dug deep into the roots of their faith and held on with courage, honesty, and love to the God who is faithful to them. One of my favorite hymns compared this kind of faith to a tree:

> There by itself like a tree it shows;
> That high it reaches as deep it goes;
> And when the storms are its branches shaking,
> It deeper root in the soil is taking.

A third principle is that a responsible fear combined with a daring faith can result in creative action. A great tragedy is that fear tends to paralyze or immobilize us. We express this all the time. "I was scared stiff." "I was so frightened I couldn't move." Fear immobilizes us. And yet, some people are able to combine that fear with a daring faith and rise up to take action.

An old fable tells the story of a lion and a goat who met at the water hole. Although there was plenty of room for both, the two began to squabble about which one should drink first, which one was strongest or wisest. The debate became so intense that they were ready to fight to the death when they looked up in the sky and saw the vultures circling overhead, waiting to come in for the kill. Seeing the vultures, they chose to drink together in the pond. Sometimes a healthy fear of the vultures will lead us toward creative, responsible action.

In the closing paragraphs of Luke 12, Jesus turns his discussion to the role of his disciples. "Be ready for whatever comes, dressed for action and with your lamps lit, like servants who are waiting for their master to come" (vv. 35-36, TEV). For Jesus the critical question is, "Who is the wise and faithful servant?" He answers his own question by saying that the wise and faithful servant is the one who is about the master's business, faithfully, loyally, consistently doing the work that the master has given the servant to do regardless of the events which might prevent it. To be a faithful servant is to be involved in creative action while the vultures are circling overhead.

Hurricane Diana swept a path of destruction across the beaches of the Carolinas. I suspect it would be fascinating to study some of the human interest stories that unfolded along its path. You would probably find neighbors who were squabbling over a property line, fighting over who had precedence in the neighborhood. You could probably find business people who were spending most of their energy undercutting each other's prices. There were no doubt couples who were seriously considering divorce, just about to throw in the towel. You might have found families who were fighting over inheritances, or over a multitude of things that families find to fight over. But then the wind began to blow; the waves began to beat against the shore; Diana began to pound the coast with its fury. Suddenly all of those things that separated and divided people became terribly unimportant as they were drawn into creative, helpful, loving, saving action in response to that storm.

Sometimes a good, healthy fear combined with faith can lead toward creative action. One example of such action has occurred in the U.S. religious community. There are multitudes in the country who are paralyzed, immobilized by the fear of nuclear destruction. But, in separate incidents, the bishops of the Catholic church and the bishops of the United Methodist church added to that responsible fear a profound biblical faith and spoke out to say it is time for the madness to end. The vultures are too close. This, of course, is a big issue, but you can apply the same principle to the small issues of your life. Responsible fear combined with daring faith can lead toward creative action.

There may be no more pervasive fear for parents of teenagers today than the fear that their son or daughter will become involved in drug abuse. This fear can be so paralyzing that it can cause parental blindness to the subtle signs of drug abuse and can lead many parents into blatant denial: "Not my son! It couldn't be him!" The fear of drug abuse immobilizes parents and makes it almost impossible for them to take action.

This was not the case, however, with two close friends who discovered that their son was heavily into marijuana and alcohol abuse. Instead of denying the painful reality before them, they took action. They faced the issue head-on with their son and placed him, against his will and at great pain to themselves, in a drug rehabilitation program. They also confronted the parents of others who had been involved in the situation. The honesty of this couple forced some of those parents out of denial and into action. It also opened the eyes of other parents to the dangerous reality of drug abuse in our neighborhood. Through them, responsible fear became creative action, and none of us will be quite the same again.

In *Moby Dick*, Starbuck, the first mate, tells his crew that he will have no one on his ship who is not afraid of the whale. Perhaps Jesus, knowing the creative forces at work through fear, is saying to us, "I will have no man or woman as my disciple who does not know what it means to be afraid."

59

Eternal God, who dwellest in the high and lofty place, yet also in him who is of an humble and a contrite heart, be to us this hour a living Presence. Be like the sun which, though it is far away, is with us in its warmth and light; like the air which though it encompasses the planet, yet is about us and within us with its vital ministries.

We come to thee because we desire liberated lives. Free us from inner tyrannies that imprison us. Deliver us from our fears. Haunted by dread and enfeebled by timidity, we make our own souls jails and our own anxieties jailers. Grant us fresh faith and new courage. Send us out with restored confidence in ourselves, our fellow men, and thee.

—Harry Emerson Fosdick

7

A NEW WAY OF SEEING

> O, wonder!
> How many goodly creatures are there here!
> How beauteous mankind is! O brave new world,
> That has such people in't!
> —William Shakespeare

Read 2 Corinthians 5:14-21

This book is about the real, measurable, identifiable difference that Jesus makes in the common, ordinary experiences of our lives. So far, we have focused primarily on the difference Jesus makes on the inside of life, our feelings and emotions. But that is only half the story. We live in a world filled with other people, people who often see reality through very different glasses than we do. It is not enough just to think about the difference Jesus makes on the inside of our souls; we also need to look at the difference he makes in our relationship with all those other people around us.

In a classic "Peanuts" cartoon, Linus confesses that while he loves humanity, it's people who give him problems. Let's face it; sometimes we are all like a bunch of porcupines with quills sticking out all over the place. I've always wondered about porcupines—how do they ever get together? Have you ever tried to hug a porcupine? Can you imagine them in a crowded elevator? Sometimes we are like that. We do fine when we have plenty of wide open space, but when we start rubbing up against each other, bumping into each other, watch out! Someone usually gets stuck.

This is Paul's concern in his second letter to Corinth. He writes: "No longer . . . do we judge anyone by human standards" (5:16, TEV). The Revised Standard Version translates that, "We regard no one from a human point of view." We no longer make value judgments about people based on how well they fit into some Madison Avenue image of what a man or woman ought to be. Rather, Paul says, "We are controlled by the love of Christ" (v. 14). The King James translation is "The love of Christ constraineth us." In Greek this is a very visceral verb that means the love of Christ grabs us by the gut and won't let us go. The love of Christ leaves us no choice. Now that we know that one man has died for all, we know that they all share in his death (v. 14). I hear Paul saying that the difference Jesus makes is that he gives us a new way of seeing all those people around us. He calls us to see other people through the eyes of the cross, to see every person as a man or woman for whom Jesus Christ died.

When I was in high school, I was dating a girl who was a profoundly stronger Christian than I. One day we went to the county fair, which, like most county fairs, had a cheap carnival midway lined with dirty little tents, each with a well-worn billboard promising much more than it could deliver. One promised "The Wild Man of the Jungle" with paintings of a ferocious-looking man fighting off wild beasts. We made the big mistake, paid twenty-five cents each, and went in.

Inside we found a low, white picket fence, and beyond the fence, a dirty, gray-haired old man sitting on the ground, fumbling around with a few harmless, half-alive garden snakes. It really turned me off! I was just about to make some foolish crack about what a fraud this was when my girlfriend turned to me with tears in her eyes and said, "Jim, just think; that is a man for whom Jesus died."

Needless to say, I had enough sense to keep my mouth shut. All I had seen was a dirty old man in a twenty-five-cent sideshow. She looked at the same man and saw a person of infinite worth, a man loved by God, a person for whom Jesus Christ died. It makes a radical difference in the way we relate to friends, co-workers, family members, husbands and wives, if we begin to see them as men and women for whom Jesus Christ died; to see them through the eyes of the cross.

Paul also says that because of Jesus, we begin to see people through the eyes of faith; we begin to see their potential, what they could become through the love of God. One of the boldest affirmations in the entire Bible is found in the seventeenth verse of this chapter: "If any one is in Christ, he is a new creation; the old has passed away, behold, the new has come" (RSV).

Christopher Cerf and Victor Navasky have written a book entitled, *The Experts Speak*, "the definitive compendium of authoritative misinformation." It contains two thousand examples of just how wrong "experts" can be. The writers record what Gary Cooper said after turning down the role of Rhett Butler, which was then given to Clark Gable: "*Gone With The Wind* is going to be the biggest flop in Hollywood history. I'm just glad it'll be Clark Gable who's falling flat on his face and not Gary Cooper." Cerf and Navasky quote the manager of the Grand Ole Opry who listened to Elvis Presley sing and gave him this advice: "You ain't goin' nowhere . . . son. You ought to go back to drivin' a truck."

One of my favorites in this kind of misinformation is the 1930s definition I once heard of *uranium*: "a white, metallic substance with no apparent value."

Isn't that often how we see other people? We only see

what they are, and we miss out on what they can become. We only see what is immediately apparent and miss their hidden potential. But look at the way Jesus relates to people in the Gospels. He is constantly seeing something there that no one else can see.

To everyone else he was just Simon, the big fisherman, a blustery, strong-willed bull in a china shop; but to Jesus, he was Peter, the "rock" upon which he would build his church.

To everyone else he was just Matthew, the tax collector, the pawn of Roman authority; but, in Christ, he became the one to write down the gospel.

To everyone else she was just a woman caught in adultery, a lawbreaker; but Jesus forgave her and told her to arise, go, and sin no more.

To everyone else he was a criminal, condemned to die on a cross; but Jesus said, "Today you will be with me in paradise."

Jesus took an over-zealous Pharisee named Saul, transformed him into Paul, and made him the greatest missionary the Christian church has ever known.

He took a country girl named Joan of Arc, gave her a vision, and made her the voice of conscience for her nation.

He took a rabble-rousing womanizer named Augustine, transformed him into a saint, and used him to help shape Christian belief.

He took an insecure, guilt-ridden priest named Martin Luther and made him the firebrand of the Reformation.

He took a black preacher's kid named Martin Luther King, Jr., and used him to set a people free.

He took a little nun from the mountains of central Europe, sent her to Calcutta, and is using Mother Teresa to teach us how to care.

"If any one is in Christ, he is a new creation; the old has passed away, behold, the new has come." It makes a profound difference in our relationships with others if we begin to see others through the eyes of faith, to see them as the persons they can become through the grace of God in Jesus Christ.

That is the difference Jesus makes in how we see others. But as Shakespeare reminded us, "The fault, dear Brutus, is not in our stars, but in ourselves." We tend to project onto others the negative, inferior, hostile feelings we have about ourselves, which is why Jesus said, "Love your neighbor as you love yourself" (Matt. 19:19, TEV). That is not so much a command as a description. You *will* treat others basically the same way you treat yourself. Most of the time our negative attitudes toward others are simply the projection of our negative feelings about ourselves.

Paul deals with how we see ourselves when he writes, "In Christ God was reconciling the world to himself, . . . and entrusting to us the message of reconciliation. So we are ambassadors for Christ, God making his appeal through us" (2 Cor. 5:19-20, RSV). It makes a tremendous difference in how we relate to others if we begin to see ourselves as ambassadors of Jesus Christ, the agents of God's reconciling love, the instruments of God's peace.

During my senior year in college, I was the president of our student body. One day I received a formal commission from the governor of Kentucky making me a member of his Student Advisory Commission. We were supposed to keep the Governor informed on what was happening on campus in the late sixties. Looking back now, I realize that the primary purpose of this commission was probably to build up steam for his reelection campaign, but I still remember climbing the steps of the capitol for the first—and come to think of it, the only—meeting of that commission. There was something exciting, something exhilarating about knowing that I was there representing my college and that I would return to the campus representing the governor. I felt that I was really somebody!

If I was that excited about representing the governor of Kentucky, how much more excited should we all feel about ourselves to hear the living Christ, the risen Lord, say to us, as he said to his first disciples, "You shall be my witnesses" (Acts 1:8, RSV). Paul says, "We are ambassadors for Christ. God was in Christ reconciling the world to himself, and now he has given us the ministry of reconciliation." We are called to be the men and women through whom the world will experience the love, the compassion, the justice, the peace of Jesus Christ.

Two of my personal heroes are Miriam and Spotty Spottswood. They spent their missionary career in the islands of the Philippines. After a long career they retired, but retirement for Spotty simply meant a change of address. Since then, he has been organizing volunteer teams of doctors, nurses, farmers, and construction workers to take their vacations and go at their own expense as Short Term Volunteers In Mission. Spotty tells the story of a young nurse who took a year's leave of absence and went to serve with him in a remote, primitive clinic on one of the islands. Most of her patients were lepers, their disease literally eating away at their flesh. About halfway through the year, a friend from the States came to visit her. The friend watched all day long as she ministered to the infected bodies of the island people. When the day was over, the friend said to her, "You know, I wouldn't do that for a million bucks!" The young nurse looked her friend in the eye and said, "You know, I wouldn't do it for a million

66

bucks either, but the love of Christ constrains me." This nurse knew what it meant to see herself as the ambassador of Christ, the agent of his healing, reconciling love.

Do you remember the story in John about the man who was born blind (9:1-25)? Jesus sees him as he and his disciples are walking along. Jesus spits on the ground, mixes the spit into clay, dabs the clay on the man's eyes, and sends him to wash in the pool of Siloam. The blind man does, and, lo and behold, when he lifts his head out of the water, he can see! When the authorities question him about it, he responds, "This is all I know, once I was blind but now I see."

There is a theory that the early church may have used this as a baptismal story. It has been found painted on the walls of the catacombs. The early Christians may have been saying: "That's what baptism is. When you accept Christ and the water is poured over your head, your eyes are opened. You have a whole new way of seeing." We begin to see people through the eyes of the cross; to see them through the eyes of faith; and to see ourselves as the agents of the reconciling love of God.

> Jesus, united by thy grace,
> And each to each endeared,
> With confidence we seek thy face,
> And know our prayer is heard.
> Help us to help each other, Lord,
> Each other's cross to bear;
> Let each his friendly aid afford,
> And feel his brother's care.
> Touched by the lodestone of thy love,
> Let all our hearts agree;
> And ever toward each other move,
> And ever move toward thee.
> —Charles Wesley

8

ENLARGING OUR BOUNDARIES

I resolved to do no business till I went to church
in the morning, but to continue pouring out my heart
before Him. And this day my spirit was enlarged.
—John Wesley

Read Luke 10:25-36, Psalm 16:5

One morning an elementary-school teacher asked her class how many points there are on the compass. She was surprised when one little boy stuck up his hand and said, "Five." "Five?" she asked. "What are they?" He counted them off, "North, south, east, west, and where I am."

This is where we all begin, right where we are. It is from those immediate perceptions that we begin to respond to the world around us. The difference in people is that some begin where they are and never go anywhere, while others begin where they are and ultimately reach around the world.

As a part of my own devotional discipline a couple of years ago, I was reading my way through the Psalms using the New English translation. I came across a verse in the Sixteenth Psalm that has stuck with me ever since. The psalmist wrote, "Thou dost enlarge my boundaries." I could identify with that. As I look at my own life, one of the specific, indentifiable differences Jesus makes is that he enlarges my boundaries. He breaks down the walls that I so carefully erect; he pulls up every fence post that I put in place. He expands my compassion and stretches my love to include people I never would have known, loved, or accepted were it not for him. He enlarges my boundaries.

I am permanently scarred and permanently blessed by the fact that I grew up in a very conservative, evangelical, WASP community. I am blessed because it gave me the roots of vital faith. I am scarred because very early in life I inherited a set of prejudices and faulty presuppositions. Most of us, wherever we have grown up, have inherited a picnic basket full of bigotry, fears, and intolerance. Whatever these were and are in your life, you can understand how shocked I was when I finally got around to meeting some of the objects of my prejudices and discovered that they were very good people. Some of them were just as deeply committed to the faith as were my forebears. In some cases they were much more profoundly biblical than the dear folks who had, perhaps unintentionally, conditioned me to reject them.

This is what the story of the Good Samaritan in Luke 10:25-37 is all about, too. One day a lawyer put a question to Jesus, the same question all of us ask sooner or later: What do I have to do to inherit eternal life? What do I have to do to find life that is so vibrant, so alive, so real that it can never be put to death?

Jesus responded with another question, "What is in the Law?" The lawyer knew the answer: " 'Love the Lord your God with all your heart, soul, mind, and strength;' and 'love your neighbor as yourself.' "

Jesus said, "You've got it! Do this and you will find life." The ball was back in the lawyer's court, and he didn't like that. He began to split hairs. "Who is my neighbor?" Again he knew the answer. It was all spelled out in the Law.

Neighbors were people just like him: good, loyal, law-abiding Jews. Neighbors were people of your own race, culture, conviction. Everyone else was an outsider. The boundaries were narrow and clear. But he asked, "Who is my neighbor?" and in so doing set Jesus up for one of the best stories in the gospel.

A certain man went down from Jerusalem to Jericho. Along the way he fell among thieves who stripped him, beat him, and left him to die. A priest and a Levite—good, law-abiding religious leaders—came along the same road, and both of them passed by on the other side. Then, along came a Samaritan. The Samaritan was clearly outside the boundaries of what a neighbor was. He was an alien, one who didn't belong. But when he saw the man, Jesus said, he was moved with compassion. The verb here comes from the root word that we would translate "viscera" or "intestines." Jesus was saying, "Something moved in this man's gut." He went over to the man, bandaged his wounds, loaded him on his own beast, took him to an inn, and stayed with him through the night. When the Samaritan left the next morning, he told the innkeeper to put the bill on his Mastercard. I can imagine the victim, waking out of his painful sleep, seeing the Samaritan riding away, saying to the innkeeper, "Who was that masked man?"

Jesus turned to the one who had asked, "Who is my neighbor?" and asked him, "Who acted like a neighbor to the man who fell among thieves?" "That's obvious," the lawyer said. "The one who showed him kindness." Jesus said, "Go and do the same things."

I suspect that if you had met that lawyer years later and asked him what difference Jesus made in his life, he might have said, "He enlarged my boundaries! He knocked down the walls. He pulled up the fence posts. He expanded my love, stretched my compassion, and gave me a whole new definition of the word *neighbor*." Jesus is still doing that today.

I once met a woman who was obviously wealthy, successful, and very intelligent. She was also a deeply committed Christian, loyal to her church, a tither, one of those people who listens to religious programs on radio and television, reads the religious periodicals, and shares her faith with those around her. She was also a hard-core racist. The love of God had not yet permeated a prejudice so deep that she told her pastor she had never touched a black person, even to shake hands, and did not intend to.

In response to a television or radio evangelist, the woman went on a mission trip to Jamaica. One of the stops was at an orphanage in a poor, remote corner of that island. The director of the orphanage told the almost unbelievable story of a little girl named Fine. As a toddler, Fine had been abandoned by her parents in the bush and left to die. Somehow, she survived on her own until she was found and brought to the orphanage. Though she was now fourteen, because of the lack of proper nutrition, she was barely four feet tall. Because of her lack of contact with other people, she was just learning to talk and could only communicate in harsh, guttural sounds.

The whole scene at that orphanage was one of the most soul-wrenching experiences in this woman's life. She said she was almost physically sick as she compared her wealth to their poverty. She was aware that she would soon return to a plush hotel on the beach but that these children would be here for the rest of their lives. She stepped out onto the porch to sort out her emotions. After a little while, she began to sense that she was not alone. She turned around and there stood Fine. Their eyes met. Fine simply lifted up her arms in the air to be held.

Something in this woman began to crack. All of her faith, all she believed about the love of God in Christ, came into direct conflict with all of her prejudice, bigotry, and racism. Hardly realizing what she was doing, she reached down, picked that child up, wrapped her arms around her, and rocked her against her breast. And the child named Fine probably wondered why the well-dressed American lady was sobbing as she held her in her arms.

Things began to change in this woman's outlook. She became much more open to and supportive of the people she had once despised. Her attitudes and her actions began to reflect the love of Christ more than the hatred of humanity. She can hardly visit her friends anymore because they can't understand the change in her. I suspect that if you asked her what difference Jesus has made in her life, she would probably say that he has enlarged her boundaries. He has torn down the walls, moved out the fences, expanded her love, enlarged her compassion to include neighbors she never knew she had before.

I think we need, now and then, to take a look at the faces of the people around us in the church, men and women whom we never would have known, relationships we never would have shared, had it not been for the love of Christ that draws us together in the faith. Then we should allow our imaginations to soar out from the place where we are to realize that we have brothers and sisters not only in Orlando, but in Ontario; not only in Miami, but in Moscow. We have kin in the family of God in Tampa and Tokyo, Boston and Berlin, Chicago and Shanghai, Houston and Havana.

The love of God revealed in the body and blood of Jesus Christ enlarges our boundaries, expands our compassion, stretches our love to include the whole world.

Eternal God, so high above us that we cannot comprehend thee and yet so deep within us that we cannot escape thee, make thyself real to us today!
We are tired of our littleness and would escape from the

narrow limitations of our ordinary lives. Lift us into the
fellowship of the saints in the light.

. . . Help us to go back to ordinary tasks to do simple
things in a redeeming way, to perform common
responsibilities with an uncommon spirit, and to face a
disordered world with triumphant souls.

—Harry Emerson Fosdick

WRESTLING IN THE WILDERNESS

> After my return home, I was much buffeted with
> temptations; but cried out, and they fled away. They
> returned again and again. I as often lifted up my
> eyes, and He "sent me help from his holy place."
> . . . I found all my strength lay in keeping my eye
> fixed upon him, and my soul waiting on him
> continually.
>
> —John Wesley

Read Luke 4:1-13, Romans 12:17-21

Come along with me in your imagination to the lonely,
desolate wilderness that stretches between the inhabited
part of Judea and the Dead Sea. In Jesus' time, it was called
Jeshimon, which means, "the Devastation." The hills are
blistered limestone formations, the rocks bare and jagged;
the ground glows with the heat of the Middle Eastern sun.
Tradition tells us that it was here that Jesus spent forty days
struggling alone with the realities of good and evil. Here he
was tempted, caught in the turmoil of conscience, strained
by the decision of who and what he would be.

I used to think this story was unique to the life of Jesus, a
story that reveals what it means to say that Jesus is the Son
of God. And it is. But in recent years, I've returned to this
wilderness and found it to be *my* story as well. I have been

there. The drama grows out of the reality of your life and mine. It is one of those stories that reveals Jesus not only as the Son of God, but also as the Son of man. He is one of us!

Like Jesus, we have been in the wilderness of temptation. Like him, we wrestle with the conflict of good and evil, the subtle temptations to compromise. In the wilderness we, like him, can begin to learn how to overcome temptation rather than be overcome by it.

Luke sets the stage for this drama by saying that Jesus was hungry. He begins with the most common, ordinary, natural human instinct we share: the desire for food. This tells us that temptation emerges out of the most common realities of our humanity. It does not come from outside our lives but from within. At its center, all temptation is the temptation to use God's good gifts in the devil's ways. It is the temptation to take good, healthy, natural, God-given instincts and misuse, distort, pervert them to our own self-serving ends.

In Luke's account, Satan says, "Jesus, look at all those limestone rocks out there. If you're really the Son of God, go ahead, turn some of those stones into bread. God doesn't want any of his children to be hungry, much less his own son! Satisfy that natural instinct. Do it for yourself" (4:3).

A contemporary version of that argument goes like this: "If it feels good, do it!" If it's a natural, physical, emotional, sexual drive within you, go ahead and satisfy it! Grab all the gusto you can! But Jesus replies, "It is written—written not only in the word, but written into the fabric of creation— 'Man cannot live only with bread' " (4:4). You are not just an animal with animal instincts and hungers; you are made for God! You are not just an animal with bodily desires and hungers; you are also a soul. Those hungers and desires can only be satisfied in God's way.

Satan tries again. This time he takes Jesus up to the

heights of human vision and shows him in a moment of time all the kingdoms of the world. He says, "Jesus, you can have it all! Money, power, wealth, prestige, success—you can have it all! All you have to do is worship me" (4:6-7).

It is as old as the Germanic legend of Faust. You can have it all. The question is, "What shall a man give in exchange for his soul? Or what shall it profit a man if he gain the whole world but lose his soul?" How much of yourself are you willing to barter away for the sake of power, prestige, and wealth? How much of your integrity will you compromise for what the world calls success? What will you worship with your life?

Jesus says, "It is written in the word and written into the character of the universe—'There is only one God worthy of your worship and you will serve him alone if you want to save your own soul'" (4:8). There are some things in this world that money can't buy. There are some things you can have, but the price is just too high.

Finally, Satan decides to try Jesus where Jesus is strongest. It is the subtle temptation that comes to the religious instincts within us. Satan takes him up on the highest point of the Temple, the symbol of the power and faith of Judaism. Then he says, "Jesus, cast yourself down off the Temple. The Ninety-first Psalm says that God will watch out for you and you won't even stub your toe on the ground" (4:9-11).

Jesus faces the subtle temptation to manipulate God, to use God for Jesus' own self-serving ends. Would you like a contemporary version of that? Listen to the electronic evangelists who promise, "If you tithe, God is going to make you rich." I believe we should tithe, but we should not do it hoping that God will make us rich because we do. Other versions are, "If I come to church, God is going to solve all my problems"; "If the preacher stands on our side, our Little League team is sure to win." We can play that out in a wide variety of terms, but it is still the same temptation to use God for our own self-serving ends.

Jesus tells Satan, "It is written—written in the word and written into the fabric of our relationship with God—'Do not put God to the test' " (4:12). You can't manipulate God. All you can do is trust and love God.

That was enough. Luke says that after Satan had tempted him in every way, every way in which you and I are tempted, he left Jesus for awhile.

These are your temptations and mine. This is our story. It grows out of the reality of our lives. The thing that stands out to me is the way Jesus overcame the power of temptation. He did not try to overcome evil by confronting it on its own turf. He overcame the power of evil by confronting it with the power of a greater good. Up against each temptation he held a greater truth, a higher affirmation, a greater good.

Temptation is like quicksand. Every Saturday afternoon matinee adventure movie worth its popcorn had a scene in which the hero and heroine were sinking in quicksand. You remember how the movie portrayed it. The more they kicked and struggled against the quicksand, the more it sucked them in. The only hope of getting out was for a friend on the land to throw a rope, tie it to the back of the four-wheel drive jeep, and pull them out. Or, perhaps they could have grabbed onto a strong branch and withstood the power that would have sucked them down.

Evil and temptation operate the same way in our lives. I don't know if St. Paul ever saw quicksand, but that is what I hear him saying to the Romans: "Hate what is evil, hold fast to what is good. . . . Do not be overcome by evil, but overcome evil with good" (12:9, 21, RSV).

Several years ago I heard Dr. William Sloane Coffin, Jr., the pastor of Riverside Church in New York City, say that there is only one thing harder than overcoming evil with good and that is to try to overcome evil with evil. If we try to overcome evil with evil, all we do is compound the total amount of evil in the world. If we try to overcome hostility with hostility, we end up with more hostility. If we try to defeat hatred with hatred, we end up with more hatred. Christians are called to love good more than they hate evil, to overcome evil with good.

Coffin's most memorable predecessor at Riverside Church, Harry Emerson Fosdick, described the same truth in these words:

> Only by a stronger passion can evil passions be expelled, and that a soul unoccupied by a positive devotion is sure to be occupied by spiritual demons. *The safety of the Master in the presence of temptation lay in his complete and positive devotion to his mission: there was no unoccupied room in his soul where evil could find a home; he knew what Dr. Chalmers called, "The expulsive power of a new affection."*

There is a powerful picture of this truth in Greek mythology. The Island of the Sirens was inhabited by beautiful women who sang such alluring songs that sailors going by the island would be drawn in and never heard from again. Ulysses had himself tied to the mast of the ship and his crew's ears filled with wax so that, no matter how strongly they wanted to give into that temptation, they would be held to the ship. Orpheus, by contrast, was the musician. His symbol was the lyre. Orpheus made such beautiful music that when he sailed by in his ship, he was not tempted by the sound of the Sirens.

There are some religious folks who believe in "negative goodness." They think the only way to overcome temptation is to be like Ulysses—to tie yourself up tight with rules and regulations or to seal your ears to the sounds of the world around you, and maybe make it through. But the story of Jesus' temptation bears witness to the power of a "positive goodness." We are not called to a negative goodness that puts life in straitjackets. We are called to a positive goodness that is so strong and so beautiful that it overwhelms the power of temptation. We can overcome evil, not by struggling with more evil, but by filling our lives with good.

A study done by the Pentagon during World War II concluded that a majority of married men in the military were unfaithful to their wives. When I read that my immediate reaction was that it was hardly news! A majority of married people in the country today are probably unfaithful to their mates. I began to think about the minority who were faithful. I am sure that some of them kept their marriage vows because of "negative goodness," afraid of disease, reprisal, or getting caught. But I can't help but believe that a larger percentage of those who were faithful did so not because of fear, but because of the positive power of a greater commitment, a higher loyalty, a profound love for the person they had married.

The only sure way to overcome temptation in our lives is to overcome it with a greater good, a higher loyalty, the positive power of the love of God in Jesus Christ. I have no idea what your point of temptation might be. That which is a stumbling block for me may be nothing more than a grain of sand for you. I do not know where your wilderness will be, but I promise that you will be tempted. You will be drawn into the wilderness, where you will wrestle with the choice of good or evil, God's way or Satan's way. The word of encouragement is this: "Hate what is evil, hold fast to what is good. . . . Do not be overcome by evil, but overcome evil with good." When temptations come, may we hear the voice of our Lord saying, "In the world you have tribulation; but be of good cheer, I have overcome the world" (John 16:33, RSV).

Almighty God, whose blessed Son was led by the Spirit to
be tempted by Satan: Come quickly to help us who are
assaulted by many temptations; and, as you know the
weaknesses of each of us, let each one find you mighty to
save; through Jesus Christ your Son our Lord, who lives
and reigns with you and the Holy Spirit, one God, now
and forever. Amen.

—The Book of Common Prayer

10

ALL THE LONELY PEOPLE

Pray that your loneliness may spur you into finding
something to live for, great enough to die for.
                                        —Dag Hammarskjöld

Read John 14:15-20, 15:11-17; Ecclesiastes 3:9-12

When was the last time you were lonely? I don't mean
alone. "Alone" is what I experience when I travel by myself
on an airplane, and I love it. I hear people tell stories about
how they sit beside someone on an airplane and hear that
person's whole life history. I don't want any of that. When I
travel, I like the anonymity, the feeling that no one knows
who I am. Now and then, all of us need the creative stillness
of being alone.

Light-years removed from being alone is being lonely.
Loneliness is that soul-wrenching pain that tears away at
the inside of my life. Loneliness is feeling that all of the
world has become a cosmic desert and I am cast out there
by myself to see whether or not I can survive. Loneliness is
the sudden stillness that comes when I have been torn away
from a person I love.

When was the last time you were lonely? For some of us,
answering that question means pulling a memory out of the

83

past. For others it is as fresh as this morning's breakfast cereal, as alive as the breath we are inhaling right now.

The writer of the Gospel of John cloaks the narrative of the Last Supper in this kind of loneliness. The story is set in the deep shadow of the coming isolation and death of Jesus, the tearing apart of his friendship with the disciples. John opens the narrative in the thirteenth chapter with these words: "Jesus knew that the hour had come for him to leave this world and to go to the Father. He had always loved those in the world who were his own, and he loved them to the very end" (v. 1, TEV).

Now the end is near. John's narrative has the feeling of a last conversation between a terminally ill patient and family, the last contact between a dying person and friends. It is almost as if John has recorded in chapters 13, 14, and 15 the "last will and testament" of Jesus. The Master bequeaths to his followers two gifts that strengthen my life when I experience this kind of loneliness.

First, Jesus promises, "I will ask the Father, and he will give you another Helper, who will stay with you forever. He is the Spirit, who reveals the truth about God. . . . When I go, you will not be left all alone; I will come back to you" (14:16-18, TEV). Jesus promises his first disciples and he promises us that we will not be left alone in this world. Just as he walked with the disciples down those dusty roads, just as he fished with them in the sea, just as he laughed at their jokes, just as he ate at their table, just as he was with them as a human being, Jesus promises that the Spirit, God's presence, will continue to be with us. This presence will be so alive, so intimate that the only way Jesus can describe it is to compare it to a vine and branches. "Remain united to me, and I will remain united to you. . . . I am the vine and you are the branches" (15:4-5, TEV).

Leslie Weatherhead was one of the leading spokesmen for the faith in Great Britain in the years surrounding

World War II. One of his most popular books was titled *The Transforming Friendship*. Weatherhead said that, when you boil it down, the Christian faith is a transforming friendship with Jesus of Nazareth, a living, dynamic relationship with this man who lived, died, and rose again two thousand years ago and whose story is told in the gospel. The point of the Christian life is to enter into that kind of renewing, revitalizing friendship. The question for us becomes, How is our friendship with Jesus? What are we doing to nurture the growth of that relationship? What are we doing to cultivate that "transforming friendship" with the spirit of Jesus Christ?

The day I stopped by to visit one of our church members, I discovered that she was having a very difficult time. Her life was filled with one tragedy after another. She told me that sometimes she woke up in the morning not knowing how she was going to face the day as she wondered what sort of tragedy would come next. But then the tension in the muscles of her face seemed to relax, her mouth began to form a smile, her eyes began to brighten, and she said, "You know what I do? Every night I sit down with my Bible; I start to read and pray, and during those times it is as if Jesus is so close I could reach out and touch him. That is what gets me through." That is exactly what Jesus promised. He gives us himself; we are never left alone.

It is a beautiful promise, but sometimes it is hard to get our fingers around it. Perhaps you have heard the story of the little boy who was afraid of the dark and didn't want to go to bed at night. Finally his mother said, "You don't have to be afraid of the dark; don't you know that God is with you?" To which he replied, "Yeah, I know that God is with me, but I'd rather have somebody with skin."

The truth is that all of us, regardless of how strong our faith may be, regardless of how independent we may believe we are, regardless of how much we cultivate that inner sense of the presence of Christ, sooner of later, want somebody with skin. So, Jesus not only bequeaths to us the Spirit; Jesus also gives us to each other. He says, "My commandment is this: love one another, just as I love you. . . . You are my friends. . . . I do not call you servants any longer" (John 15:12, 14-15, TEV). He gives himself to us and then he gives us to each other as friends.

Sometimes the most obvious things in life are the easiest to miss. One of them is that, if we say we believe in Jesus and are his followers, we are given to each other in love; we are called to a ministry of friendship. I didn't choose that—it was given to me. I chose to be a follower of Jesus Christ and all of you came in with the bargain. If you choose to be a follower of Jesus Christ, you get all the rest of us with him. We are brothers and sisters in the family of God. As a college student, I heard E. Stanley Jones say that everyone who belongs to Christ belongs to everyone who belongs to Christ. We belong to each other.

This idea was not new with Jesus. It is in this Old Testament passage from Ecclesiastes: "Two are better off than one. . . . If one of them falls down, the other can help him up. But if someone is alone and falls, it's just too bad, because there is no one to help him. . . . Two can sleep together and stay warm, but how can you keep warm by yourself?" (4:9-11, TEV). We are given to one another. We are called to the ministry of friendship.

When cold weather comes and we move toward the end of the year, one of the things that I remember out of my past is that this was inventory time in my father's auto parts warehouse. It was in the days before computers, which meant that when I got home from school I would go to work in the warehouses, counting by hand every one of those tail pipes, mufflers, and spark plugs. We had to take inventory every year; we counted up everything in the store to see how we came out. As I thought about this passage from Ecclesiastes, I began taking inventory of the history of the church of which I am a part and that I helped to organize. I remembered some phrases, some words that were very significant to us when we were in the process of projecting the future of this new congregation. Phrases like, "We want to be a healing community where men and women find healing for broken lives and broken relationships." We said we wanted to be a family where people felt like brothers and sisters in the love of God. We used words like care, support, encouragement, and compassion. One of our members designed our own paraphrase of the nineteenth and twenty-second verses of Ephesians 2 into a cornerstone, and we laid the stone into the center of the patio floor where it is central to all that we do: "You are no longer strangers but you are members of the family of God . . . being built together into a place where God lives."

I took inventory on those hopes. How are we doing? Where have we come? Frankly, I felt pretty good about it. I realized that, six years later, we still measure the success of this congregation not in terms of the raw number of people who come through the door, not in terms of the number of members on the roll, but in terms of relationships. How many folks have new friends they never would have had if they had not been drawn together by the love of Christ in this church? Are there people who are caring about each other, laughing together, playing together, visiting in each other's homes who never would have been drawn into a relationship if they hadn't found each other in this church? How many people are involved in small groups—Sunday school classes, Bible study groups, prayer groups, growth groups, ministry groups, prayer breakfasts, women's groups? We are not perfect; we still have a way to go. But I remember the stories, the faces of people who have been drawn together by nothing more than their common faith in Christ.

I have been given a number of books. Some are helpful for study; some help fill shelves. One of my shelf-fillers is a compendium of quotations, called *The New Dictionary of Thoughts*. I looked up *loneliness* and expected to find page after page of quotations. I only found one, a sentence by Joseph Fort Newton that reads, "People are lonely because they build walls instead of bridges." That is really all you need to say about loneliness. We are adept at building walls. I wonder how effective we are at building bridges?

My neighbor has had a very difficult year. His wife has been in the hospital three times for major surgery. She has been at home as a semi-invalid for more of the year. They haven't been able to go to their church. One Friday I was out in my yard when he came by and we talked, as we often do, about each other's churches. He told me about a neighborhood gathering for the members of their church who live in our area. They were going because she could travel in the neighborhood. Then he said to me, "You know, Jim, it's been a tough year. I don't think we could have made it without good Christian friends, but that's made it all okay. We're going to be fine."

Jesus said, "You're no longer servants; you are friends." We are given to one another in his love. He bequeaths to us, out of his own loneliness, two gifts: the gift of the Spirit and the gift of each other. That is the difference Jesus makes when I am lonely.

> Large was his bounty, and his soul sincere;
>   Heaven did a recompense as largely send:
> He gave to misery all he had, a tear;
>   He gained from heaven ('twas all he wished) a friend.
>   —Thomas Gray

11

GIANTS AND GRASSHOPPERS

> There stood a man who could look no way but
> downwards, with a muckrake in his hand. There
> stood also one over his head with a celestial crown in
> his hand, and he proffered him that crown for his
> muckrake; but the man did neither look up nor
> regard, but raked to himself the straws, the small
> sticks, and the dust of the floor.
>
> —John Bunyan

Read Numbers 13–14, Matthew 14:13-21

One sunny summer morning in 1980, the readers of *The Orlando Sentinel Star Sunday Magazine* were greeted by a cover drawing of a gigantic cockroach devouring the skyline of downtown Orlando. This introduced an article entitled "The Bug That Took Florida," a gory if not glorious tribute to the most durable resident of the Sunshine State. The article confirmed what we already suspected: exterminators not withstanding, cockroaches are here to stay! They've been here a million or so years and will probably be here a million more.

The sentence that particularly snagged my attention quoted a local exterminator named Paul "The Bug Man" Warren, who said that he concentrates on learning to think like a cockroach. He said, "I think, 'Where would I hide if you were looking for me?' "

You have probably not spent a great deal of time trying to think like a cockroach, but what the Bug Man attempts is not far removed from the biblical story of Caleb and Joshua, and not far removed from something many of us experience every day.

Having reached the border of the Promised Land, the children of Israel send a team of spies on a reconnaissance mission. When the spies return and give their report to Moses and the people, all twelve spies agree on two things. First, they agree that it is indeed a good, fertile land, flowing with milk and honey. Second, they agree that the inhabitants are strong, the cities large and well-fortified. The spies differ, however, on their conclusions. The majority recommendation is pessimistic: "We are not able to go up against the people; for they are stronger than we" (Num. 13:31, RSV). They describe the land as one that devours its inhabitants and they call the people giants. Their most revealing statement is in Numbers 13:33: "We seemed to ourselves like grasshoppers" (RSV).

They have, it seems, accomplished what the Bug Man attempts: they have learned to think like insects. Their problem is not so much the giants in the land as the grasshoppers in their minds. It is not so much a problem of the circumstances without as of their attitude, their spirit, their identity within. They have convinced themselves that they are not big enough, strong enough, powerful enough to take possession of the Promised Land.

Reflecting on this passage, Dr. William Sloane Coffin, Jr., said, "Fear distorts the truth not by exaggerating the ills of the world—which would be difficult—but by underestimating our ability to deal with them." A strong dose of fear, born out of a feeling of inferiority, stifles the confidence of the majority.

TO DO WHAT GOD HAS LEAD THEM TO DO.

But there is also a minority report offered by Caleb. He does not deny that the land is filled with strong people who live in well-fortified cities. But looking at the same situation he says, "Let us go up at once, and occupy it; for we are well able to overcome it" (Num. 13:30, RSV). In response to the discouraging report of the other spies, Caleb cries out, "The land is an exceedingly good land. If the Lord delights in us, he will bring us into this land and give it to us" (14:7-8, RSV). He concludes his speech with this bold affirmation: "The Lord is with us; do not fear them" (14:9, RSV).

Predictably, the people accept the majority report. We read, "All the congregation raised a loud cry; and the people wept that night. And all the people of Israel murmured against Moses and Aaron; the whole congregation said to them, 'Would that we had died in the land of Egypt!' . . . And they said to one another, 'Let us choose a captain, and go back to Egypt' " (14:1-2, 4, RSV).

What a tragic commentary on the story of the Exodus! The chosen people refuse to choose their destiny; the people of the promise are ready to give up on the promise of God; instead of going forward to the freedom to which God had called them, they were ready to go back to the slavery from which God had liberated them. God, however, votes on the side of the minority! "None of those who have rejected me will ever enter [the Promised Land]. But because my servant Caleb has a different attitude and has remained loyal to me, I will bring him into the land" (14:23-24, TEV).

It was that "different attitude" that set Caleb apart. Looking at the same set of circumstances, ten of the spies said, "We are like grasshoppers. We cannot take the land." But Caleb said, "The Lord is with us. We are well able. We have nothing to fear."

This story is just as real, just as practical, just as true to human experience today as it was the first time it was told.

In every day, in every age, in every situation, there are those who look at the opportunities around them and say, "We are grasshoppers in a land of giants. They will devour us. We cannot do it." But there are also folks who look at the same set of circumstances and say, "We are able! Let us go up at once and occupy the Promised Land! The Lord is with us! We have nothing to fear!"

How we see ourselves in relationship to the circumstances around us is at the heart of what the gospel says it means to live by faith. Do you remember the story of the feeding of the five thousand? It was such a formative picture of the ministry of Jesus that it became one of only a few stories to appear in all four of the Gospels. Simply put, the disciples faced an impossible situation. It was evening; they were in an isolated, lonely place; it was time to eat, and they had five thousand hungry mouths to feed. The disciples told Jesus to send the people into the villages to buy food. Can you imagine how surprised they must have been when Jesus said, "They don't have to leave. . . You yourselves give them something to eat!" (Matt. 14:16, TEV). How could Jesus even suggest such a thing? They replied, "All we have here are five loaves and two fish" (Matt. 14:17, TEV). They might as well have said, "Jesus, you've got to be kidding! We can't take care of this kind of crowd. This is a giant situation, and we only have grasshopper resources."

But Jesus took what they had, gave thanks to God for it, and used their limited resources to meet the need of the vast crowd of people. Not only did everyone get enough to eat, but they took up twelve baskets full of what was left over.

Don't try to explain this miracle. The early church didn't. This story is not here because they could explain how it happened. I believe this story held a strong place in the experience of early Christians because they knew they were facing an impossible task. How could they ever feed the multitude? How could they fulfill the call Christ had placed upon their lives? How could they enter the world to make disciples? That was a giant task and their resources seemed so small. By all human standards, they were grasshoppers in a land of giants. But they kept telling this story to remind themselves that Jesus was able to take whatever they had to give and use it beyond anything they could imagine. The story became the living picture of their confident faith that God is able to take weakness and turn it into strength; God is able to take limited resources and use them for unlimited good; God is able to take the common loaves and fishes of our lives and multiply them to meet the need of multitudes. There very well may be giants in the land; from a human point of view the odds may be stacked against us, but, "The Lord is with us. We are well able. We have nothing to fear."

It was this kind of confident faith that kept St. Paul going through all the frustrations, detours, delays, and disappointments of his ministry. Listen to his own witness from his letter to Philippi: "I have learned to find resources in myself whatever my circumstances. I know what it is to be brought low, and I know what it is to have plenty. I have been very thoroughly initiated into the human lot with all its ups and downs—fullness and hunger, plenty and want. I have strength for anything through him who gives me power" (4:11-13, NEB). Perhaps you memorized that thirteenth verse as a youth from the King James translation: "I can do all things through Christ who strengtheneth me." It is the bold affirmation of a confident relationship with Christ that broke the bondage of inferiority and set the apostle free to fulfill his calling, to claim the promise, to choose his destiny as a follower of Jesus Christ.

The obvious question that these biblical stories place before us is simply this: Which attitude is motivating and driving you? Do you struggle under the bondage of inferiority? Do you look at the opportunities, challenges,

responsibilities that are before you and say, "There are
giants in the land and I feel like a grasshopper"? Or do you,
like Caleb, look across into some new Promised Land full of
risk, danger, and possibilities and say, "We are well able;
the Lord is with us; we have nothing to fear"?

None of us who were involved in our summer camping
program will be able to forget Alyce. She was the only
dwarf I have ever known. I first met her when she came as a
junior high camper. She stands just barely above my waist.
The first sixteen years of her life were an unending series of
painful operations on her legs, and she was told as a child
that she would probably never walk. Life is a long story of
potential frustrations for her. Water fountains are all too
high. Public telephones used to be a total impossibility. To
keep up with long-legged people like me while walking
means that she almost has to run. She makes all of her own
clothing because she can't buy anything that will fit. I must
confess that the first time I saw her as a camper, I really
wondered why she had come to camp. There seemed to be
so much she couldn't do. But at that time I did not really
know Alyce. All I could see were the things that I thought
she could not do. I did not see all the things she could do:
her contagious joy; her faith; her love; and, most of all, her
indomitable spirit.

I missed one year at camp. The next summer when I
returned, Alyce was a member of the Youth Leadership
Team. When you think of the team, you picture rugged
athletes serving as lifeguards, cabin counselors, recreation
leaders. But here was Alyce. Every morning she would
bounce onto a stool behind the registration desk where she
worked in the morning. She tended the camp store in the
afternoon. In between, you would find her painting, working with crafts, and just talking with some lonely kid who
didn't feel worth very much. The last time I saw Alyce, she
was ready to graduate from college. She wanted to be a

teacher. And you know, I believe she will make it! She refused to say, "I am not able." With Caleb of old, her life shouts, "We are able! Let us go up and occupy the land. The Lord is with us!"

> With all the resources of an infinite God available to them that ask Thee, forgive us, O Lord, for our lack of faith that begs for pennies when we could write checks for millions; that strikes a match when we could have the sun. Give to us the faith to believe that there is no problem before us that Thy wisdom cannot solve. . . . Amen.

—Peter Marshall

12

WHAT ONE PERSON CAN DO

> The voice of a single individual . . . would have
> prevented this abominable crime [of slavery] from
> spreading itself over the new country. Thus we see
> the fate of millions unborn hanging on the tongue of
> one man, and Heaven was silent in that awful
> moment! But it is to be hoped it will not always be
> silent, and that the friends to the rights of human
> nature will in the end prevail.
> > —Thomas Jefferson, after an act of
> > Congress abolishing slavery in
> > the territories was defeated by
> > one vote in 1784.

Read 1 Corinthians 1:18-31, 2 Corinthians 4:7

One of my favorite musicians and one of the prophetic
voices of our time is John Denver. To celebrate the eighty-
fifth birthday of R. Buckminster Fuller, he wrote a song that
goes:

> What one man can do is dream.
> What one man can do is love.
> What one man can do is change the world
> And make it work again.
> Here you see what one man can do.

This has an important word for us. In a day of mega-

trends, megabucks, and megaproblems, we may be tempted to feel terribly insignificant, to think that there is little or
nothing any one of us can do about the world in which we
live. Denver's song is a powerful affirmation of the inherent
dignity and strength of those people who allow their lives to
make a difference. "Here you see what one man can do."

The date was October 31, 1517. A young monk named
Martin Luther marched up to the castle chapel in Witten-
berg, Germany, and nailed the Ninety-five Theses to the
door. His purpose in this was to begin a debate on specific
practices in the Roman Catholic church. Little did he
realize that this act would set fire to a Reformation that
would change the entire course of Western history. It was
like a missile that, once set off, could never be recalled. We
still live in the fallout of what Martin Luther did.

It is important to realize that Luther's act was more an
act of conscience than an act of rebellion. He had simply
discovered through his own study of scripture and through
his own experience of faith an important fact that all of us
find so easy to forget: we are not saved by anything we do or
don't do, by anything we earn or merit, much less by the
authority of the church. Luther rediscovered that we are
saved by the outrageous grace of God.

I choose that adjective *outrageous* because the dictionary
says it means, "Going beyond the bounds of moderation."
What Luther rediscovered and what we constantly need to
rediscover in our own day is that we are saved by that
amazing grace that goes completely beyond the bounds of
moderation. It is given to us a free gift of God. All we can do
is receive it and live responsibly within it.

Luther never intended to begin a reformation. He was
simply a man whose conscience was captive to the Word of
God. He had no choice: he had to act on his conscience; but
once the Reformation began, it could not be stopped. As a
matter of fact, there came a time when Luther would have

liked to have held it back, but could not do it. A singularly insignificant act was used by God in a surprisingly significant way.

Perhaps this was what Paul had in mind when he wrote to common, ordinary people who had responded to the gospel and said, "Remember what you were . . . when God called you. Few of you were wise or powerful or of high social standing" (1 Cor. 1:26, TEV). In other words, the Christians in Corinth were a motley crew, just like that motley crew of tax collectors, fishermen, and day laborers whom Jesus called to be his first disciples. They weren't anybody special—just earthy, ordinary folk. But Paul said, "God purposely chose what the world considers nonsense in order to shame the wise, and he chose what the world considers weak in order to shame the powerful. He chose what the world looks down on and despises and thinks is nothing, in order to destroy what the world thinks is important" (1 Cor. 1:27-28, TEV). In his second letter to the Corinthians, Paul wrote, "We have this treasure in earthen vessels, to show that the transcendent power belongs to God and not to us" (4:7, RSV).

Strange as it may seem, God chooses to be at work in human history through common, ordinary, earthy sinners like Martin Luther and you and me. God chooses to give the treasures of goodness, grace, mercy, and peace to this world through ordinary men and women who discover that their consciences have become captive to the word of God and who simply do what they know they must do to live with their consciences. Through people like this, the kingdoms of this earth actually have a fighting chance of becoming the kingdoms of our God and of Christ. Here you see what one person can do.

Think about Stephen, the first martyr of the Christian faith. Stephen never intended to be a hero. All Stephen knew was that he could not live with himself if he did not bear witness to what he had experienced in Jesus Christ. He told his story and was stoned for it (Acts 6:8–7:60). While the stones were falling on his head, I suspect Stephen figured that it was all over and that it hadn't amounted to very much at all. There was no way that Stephen could have guessed that God had a man named Saul over at the edge of the crowd, holding the coats of those who were working up such a sweat stoning him. Stephen could not have known that watching him die would be the beginning of the process of transformation in Saul's life so that Saul would become Paul and human history would never be the same. Here you see what one person can do.

In AD 391, a Christian named Telemachus became concerned about the depravity of the Roman Empire, the bloodthirsty craving for violence, the gladiators, the Colosseum, the arena. Some of this is not that far removed from the bloodthirsty craving of our society for violent entertainment. Finally Telemachus could be silent no longer. He jumped out of the stands in the arena in Rome, stood in front of the crowd, lifted his arms in the air, and said, "In the name of God, stop this madness!" The crowd turned on Telemachus and killed him. Telemachus never could have guessed that the Emperor Honorius would be so disturbed by that incident that in a very short time he would sign the imperial edict that ended the brutality of those games.

When I heard the story of Telemachus and thought about the increasing violence and brutality of the society in which we live and of the escalating insanity of the nuclear arms race, something in me asked, "Isn't it time for some Christian somewhere to take the risk of saying, 'In the name of God stop this madness'?" Here you see what one person can do.

A twenty-six-year-old Englishwoman in 1846 was struggling in her conscience with what God would have her do with her life. She recorded this prayer, "O God, Thou puttest into my heart this great desire to devote myself to the sick and sorrowful." Later she prayed, "Give me my work to do." God gave her work to do, but who would have ever predicted that Florence Nightingale's work in the filthy hospital barracks of the Crimean War would transform everything that we understand of hospital and nursing care? She simply did what she believed God had called her to do. Here you see what one person can do.

It was December 1, 1955. A black seamstress named Rosa Parks was on her way home from work. She was tired and her feet hurt as she climbed onto a bus in Montgomery, Alabama. At the next stop, a white man came onto the bus. Following the common practice of the day, the bus driver told Rosa Parks she would have to stand so that he could expand the white seating area for this white businessman to sit down. Rosa Parks later said that all she knew was that she was tired and she had had enough. She said, "No," and refused to move, never guessing that God had a preacher named Martin Luther King, Jr., around the corner at Dexter Avenue Baptist Church and that her simple act of conscience would be the spark that would ignite a reformation that has changed the social fabric of America. Here you see what one person can do.

J. B. Kenyon had retired long before I came to Asbury College. Although every student on campus saw his name carved above the entrance to Kenyon Library, there were only a few who actually got to know him. They would meet him when he was walking across the campus on his way to chapel. It was a habit, born out of his ten college generations as a teacher and then dean, a habit that he continued in retirement because it had meaning for him and because he never lost his love of campus life. The old man would pause along the way to wink at a young couple with their arms around each other on a green park bench, to encourage a student who looked depressed, to pick up a piece of paper that was littering the campus. Those who knew him in those final years of his life knew that he still laughed, still listened, still loved, still cared.

He died during my senior year. As president of the student government, I was called upon to speak in chapel of his influence. Though I tried to find my own words, I finally decided that I could not improve on the description recorded in the college yearbook that was dedicated to him the year of his retirement:

> Yours has been a simple message executed with faithfulness. In tomorrow-years the halls will sound with the laughter of another student body. Perhaps they will know you only as a name. . . . But more, they will hear of a man who was never too busy to flash a smile at a homesick Freshman, or too busy to listen to a student's problem, or too busy to be friendly in a way that is more than friendly. They may never see the twinkle in your eye, but they will see it in the eye of the one who speaks of you. . . . We will remember you, the silver-headed man whose spirit and life represent to us all that our [college] is.

He was a quiet, simple, silver-headed man, but here you see what one person can do.

Look around the community, the neighborhood, the family in which you live. Look at the ordinary people who live and act on the basis of their Christian consciences. Who would ever be able to predict what God might do with those simple acts of obedience? You have no idea who might be growing up next to you, who God may have waiting in the wings to be a part of God's purpose in history.

I can't explain God's methods. Sometimes they make absolutely no sense to me. Sometimes I think God is highly mistaken in the way things operate. But the evidence is that, to paraphrase Paul, God chooses what the world considers to be weakness to shame what the world considers to be power; God chooses what the world thinks of as nonsense to shame what the world thinks is wise. God chooses simple, insignificant men and women whose consciences have become captive to the word and uses them to accomplish God's mysterious, creative, redemptive purpose in the world.

The subtle problem with the title of this chapter is in the subject of its verb: what one *person* can do. The important thing in human history is not what one man or one woman does; the important thing is what *God* can do through all men and women who choose to be available; who allow their lives, their minds, and their consciences to be shaped by the spirit of Jesus Christ; who are willing to live out that life in their own day and their own time. To remind us of this, St. Paul concludes by saying, "No one can boast in God's presence. . . . God has brought you into union with Jesus Christ, and God has made Christ to be our wisdom" (1 Cor. 1:29-30, TEV), the one who shapes our conscience. "Whoever wants to boast must boast of what the Lord has done" (1 Cor. 1:31, TEV).

Here you see what God can do through any man or woman who is available to God, who allows the "earthen vessel" of his or her life to be filled with the transcendent glory of God.

> *Before* Thee, Father,
>> In righteousness and humility,
>
> *With* Thee, Brother,
>> In faith and courage,
>
> *In* Thee, Spirit,
>> In stillness.
>
> *Thine*—for Thy will is my destiny,
> *Dedicated*—for my destiny is to be used and used up according to Thy will.
>
> —Dag Hammarskjöld

13 ————————————

SOUL DRAIN AND
RESOURCES FOR RECOVERY

As I plunge deeper, in fits and starts, seeking to
penetrate the mystery of God, the mystery grows. It
grows in wonder and in power, in moment and in
depth. There are times of distraction, fragmentation,
alienation, and brokenness when God is not with
me. But when I open myself to God, my wholeness
is restored.

—F. Forrester Church

Read Ephesians 3:14-19

"Soul drain." Though you probably will not find the
term in a medical dictionary, it may be one of the most
widespread epidemics in the United States today. More
common than the common cold, as dangerous as drug
abuse, as difficult to cure as cancer, it is a vicious malaise of
the spirit, the draining of our inner resources, the emptiness
of shattered hopes, the darkness of disappointed dreams.
Soul drain is what remains on the other side of those
experiences that burn up all the energy we have, leaving us
to feel like a propane gas tank that has run dry—hollow,
empty, weightless except for an empty shell. Comedian Flip
Wilson says that although beauty may be only skin deep,
"ugly" goes all the way to the bone. Soul drain is that

weariness of the mind and will that goes all the way to the bone.

I first heard soul drain described in an address by Dr. Maxie Dunnam to the United Methodist Men of Florida. The phrase stuck with me; it made sense. In fact, I borrowed it right away for an article in the religion section of our local newspaper. But it was some time later that I experienced it in all its awesome power.

My whole family knew Dad's death was coming. Together we had faced the brutal fact of the inoperable tumor in his brain. Together we talked of life and death and life beyond death. Together we planned his memorial service. Together we resolved old conflicts and forgave old wounds. It was by all human standards a "good death."

But even when it is "good," death is still "the last enemy" (1 Cor. 15:26). It leaves us shattered, stunned, broken, alone. As I flew back to Pennsylvania to lay my father's body to rest in his native soil, I found myself facing the full weight of soul drain and began searching for resources for my own recovery. I will explain what I found.

First, I found healing power of the reaffirmation of mystery. Our contemporary society has tried somewhat successfully to sweep mystery under the rug of science and technology. Have you heard the twentieth-century version of "Twinkle, Twinkle Little Star"? It goes like this:

> Twinkle, twinkle little star,
> We know exactly what you are.
> We've got your size, we know your mass.
> You're not a star; you're helium gas.

We want to cut everything down to our size, squeeze every experience into the test tube of our own understanding. But there is infinitely more to life than that. John Killinger opened my own thinking with these words: "Mystery is the true order of things. A *wildness* lies in wait, as G. K. Chesterton once said. Our mathematics was not wrong, but too small. Truth is not necessarily *other* than what modern man has discovered, but it is *more* than he has discovered."

What is death, after all, if it is not the ultimate mystery of life? Who can fully explain it? Scientific knowledge can explain the biological process or analyze the cause, but who can fully explain how at one moment, even with sickness or pain, a person is alive, somehow present with us; but a moment later, life is gone. The body becomes an empty shell. It is a mystery that goes beyond all of our scientific explanations.

And who can explain eternal life? We doubt, question, probe, but the history of the human race reveals that most of us most of the time cannot help but believe in life after death. St. Paul got about as close as any of us can when he said, "Lo! I tell you a mystery. We shall not all sleep, but we shall all be changed" (1 Cor. 15:51, RSV).

We walked back to the cemetery as the sun was setting on the day of my father's funeral. I looked down at the loosely packed soil and saw in my mind's eye the body, encased in its coffin and sealed in the vault, buried beneath the ground. I turned to my wife and said, "If I really thought this was all there is, if I really thought that all there was of Dad is buried here, I'd probably crack up, too." I could understand why death destroys some folks. But in that moment, and in the days that have followed, I have never doubted the mystery of eternal life. I can explain death in sensible ways in which I cannot explain eternal life—it is a mystery—but I find strength in the mystery of eternal life that scientific explanations of death can never provide.

Second, I discovered resources for recovery in spiritual discipline. In 1980, George Gallup, Jr., published the results of a major study of Americans' attitudes on faith and religion. He discovered several areas of concern, among

107

which he described a lack of spiritual discipline. He wrote that Christians "want the fruits or reward of faith, but seem to dodge the responsibilities and obligations." His research confirmed what most of us already know: if we are to have adequate inner resources to meet the demands of life, we will need to develop our spiritual discipline.

Watch the runners in the Boston Marathon. The ability to make it up Heartbreak Hill and down into the Prudential Center is a direct result of stamina and strength developed through physical training and discipline. The same principle applies to the strength of our faith. The depth of our inner resources to cope with soul drain is in direct proportion to the spiritual discipline we practice along the way.

As I began to recover from my bout with soul drain, I drew deeply on the faith resources that were planted within my soul across years of on-again, off-again spiritual discipline. For example, the home and church in which I grew up were singing circles of faith. We were nurtured in the faith as it is expressed in old, favorite hymns and songs. So much so, that when it came time to choose hymns for my father's memorial service, the most difficult task was selecting which ones we would use. Tunes and words that had been unintentionally memorized by constant use emerged from the basement of memory to give hope, peace, and the promise of renewed strength.

I experienced the same process with familiar passages of scripture, implanted in the memory by years of exposure, that emerged as a resource for strength and hope when they were needed. Do you remember the last words of Jesus, spoken as life slipped away from him in the agony of crucifixion? Most of them are drawn directly from the Old Testament, verses that were embedded in his soul during those unrecorded years as he grew up in Nazareth, memorized in preparation for his bar mitzvah, heard in the Torah readings in the synagogue, repeated by his parents in their home. Through years of discipline, the word was so deeply planted within his personality that even as he died, the word came forth as a source of inner strength. Jesus' experience is a model of the way spiritual discipline becomes a resource for recovery from soul drain.

The ministry of friendship was the third resource I discovered. In his letter to Ephesus, St. Paul prays that the early Christians know "the Spirit's inner reinforcement" (3:16). Two verses later he uses this fascinating phrase: "together with all God's people" (3:18, TEV). He is expressing what those who have come through soul drain already know. It is in fellowship with other Christians that we most often experience the strengthening power of God's spirit. There are some things we can and must do for ourselves. There are other things that can only happen through the shared life of the community of faith. It is where two or three are gathered together that we experience the presence of Christ.

We all gathered back home, back in the small town where Dad was born, where he lived and worked and where he died. As the news of his death spread, people came with their covered dishes of Jell-O and ham salad. The phone rang, the cards came in the mail, and friends were with us, all the way to the grave. All of them gave, in their own way, the gifts of love, gratitude, and friendship. Through these gifts came the gift of healing.

When Sam Rayburn was diagnosed as having a terminal disease, he surprised his colleagues in the Senate by refusing the medical facilities of Washington and choosing to go home to Bonham, Texas. When asked why, he said that Bonham, Texas, was the kind of place where they cared when you were sick and they knew when you died. All of us look for that kind of place; a place where we find the spirit's inner reinforcement through the ministry of friendship.

Soul drain. Beyond that phrase, there is only one thing I

remember from Maxie Dunnam's address on the subject. He asked the laymen, "Does religion help when the bottom falls out?" He then answered his own question. "It depends on your religion. It depends on the image of God you carry into the darkness." Having faced the darkness, I rejoice in the assurance that Jesus Christ does make a difference, that the faith provides resources for recovery from soul drain.

> I praise you, Lord, because you have saved me.
> . . . .
> I was on my way to the depths below,
>   but you restored my life.
> Sing praise to the Lord,
>   all his faithful people!
> Remember what the Holy One has done,
>   and give him thanks!
> His anger lasts only a moment,
>   his goodness for a lifetime.
> Tears may flow in the night,
>   but joy comes in the morning.
> . . . .
> You have changed my sadness into a joyful dance;
>   you have taken away my sorrow
>   and surrounded me with joy.
> —Psalm 30:1, 3-5, 11, TEV

14

WHO'S AFRAID OF THE BIG, BAD WOLF?

> It is so wonderful to know that despite today's chill
> and yesterday's bluster, spring is here. Energy is
> pouring out of the ground and into every blade of
> grass, every crocus, magnolia bush and cherry tree.
> Soon the robins will join the pigeons, the sky will be
> full of the thunder of the sun. . . . Overhead and
> underfoot and all around we shall soon see, hear, feel
> and smell the juice and joy of spring.
>   Likewise, it is wonderful to know that despite
> appearances to the contrary, this is an Easter world.
> —Dr. William Sloane Coffin, Jr.

Read John 11:17-44, Revelation 7:9-17

I can still hear the song, its cheerful melody embedded
in my memory by long hours in front of an old 78 RPM
record player, its images painted in my imagination long
before MTV began creating them for us. It told the story of
three little pigs, preparing their houses for the onslaught of
the big, bad wolf. The first time we hear the song, it is on the
lips of the two little pigs who built their houses out of sticks
and straw. They sing with foolhardy bravado, "Who's afraid of the big, bad wolf? Tra, la, la, la, la."

But that is before they see the wolf. In due time, the wolf
comes. The pigs face it in all its awesome, destructive fury.
A few huffs and puffs and their foolhardy bravado is blown

111

away with their homes. They huddle with the third little pig in the third pig's house of bricks. Again the wolf comes to their doorstep. Again it huffs and puffs, attempting to blow the house down, but this time it simply huffs and puffs itself right out of existence.

They sing the song again, but it's different now. Instead of foolhardy bravado, it is a song of celebration, the kind of song that comes on the other side of tragedy. It is the exuberant song of three little pigs who have seen the wolf at its worst but have come through on the other side. It's like the joyfulness of white-robed saints and martyrs pictured in Revelation, gathered around the throne of God, singing, "Salvation comes from God!" It's like the laughter of Lazarus, looking back at an empty tomb.

Every person who lives in the public eye needs a friend like Lazarus, the kind of friend with whom you can kick off your shoes, let down your hair, be just who you are without having to worry about how it is going to look on the front page of the morning paper or how it is going to sound on the evening news. The evidence is that Lazarus was that kind of friend for Jesus. The home in which Lazarus and his two sisters lived was that kind of refuge for our Lord. Jesus needed Lazarus, loved him, liked him, the way each of us needs, loves, likes, a "best friend."

But Lazarus is dead and Jesus has come back to Bethany to stand by the grave of his friend. As John tells the story, it is filled with all sorts of things we may not fully understand, but it is also filled with real human emotions that all of us know and feel. There is human sorrow here. Can you think of a more poignant picture in the New Testament than this picture of Jesus weeping beside the grave of his friend? If Jesus cries beside the grave of his friend, then I can cry there, too.

There is anger in this story, the kind of righteous anger that all of us feel in the face of death. Mary and Martha

112

both throw themselves into Jesus' arms, I suspect pounding their fists on his chest, crying, "Lord, if you had only been here, our brother wouldn't have died!" Lazarus's neighbors and friends say what we would say: "He gave sight to blind people, didn't he? Couldn't he have kept his friend from dying?"

The answer, of course, is no. Sooner or later, with or without the presence of Jesus, Lazarus was going to die. Sooner or later, we all face our own mortality and even the Son of God cannot keep that wolf from our door.

In his book *Telling the Truth*, Frederick Buechner describes the gospel in terms of tragedy and comedy. He says that we weep with Jesus beside the grave of Lazarus because we know that tragedy is inevitable. Given who we are, given the weakness of our human flesh, given the tragic warp of sin, death is inevitable. This is exactly what we have come to expect. But grace surprises us, the same way a good comedy surprises us with that which is unforseen, unexpected. It catches us off guard. The surprise is that God gives us that which we have no reason to expect: laughter in the face of sorrow, hope in the face of fear, life in the face of death.

Like us, Jesus weeps beside the tomb. Then he asks the attendants to roll away the stone from the entrance. Ever-practical Martha says, "Lord, there will be a terrible stench because he's been dead for four days!" It may sound crude, but that is an intelligent, reasonable thing to say. That is predictable. It is exactly what everyone has a right to expect. But Jesus says, "Didn't I tell you that you would see the glory of God if you believe in me?" Which is at least to say, "Trust me and even the stench of death can be used for the glory of God. Trust me and the darkness of the tomb can be filled with inextinguishable light. Trust me and even the dead can be given new life."

Expecting the worst and holding their breath, they roll

the stone away. Then Jesus calls into the darkness, "Lazarus, come forth!" The unexpected happens: to everyone's surprise, he comes out, dragging his grave clothes behind him, looking for all the world like Boris Karloff in *The Mummy*. But he is alive! The inevitability of death has been broken by the unexpected, unforeseen grace of God!

One of the oldest Easter hymns captured the feeling of this moment:

> The powers of death have done their worst,
> But Christ their legions hath disbursed,
> Let shouts of holy joy outburst:
> Alleluia!

The point of the story is not that Jesus protects us from death. He doesn't; we will all die. This is inevitable, predictable. The point is that, because of what Jesus does with death, I do not have to be afraid anymore. The key to the story is verses 25 and 26, in which Jesus says, "I am [present tense] the resurrection and the life; he who believes in me, though he die [that's predictable, inevitable] yet shall he live [that's the surprise, the unexpected gift of grace], and whoever lives and believes in me shall never die" (RSV).

Through the experience of being with people when they die and through my father's death, I came to a conclusion about death. I cannot mark it on the calendar, but I can remember saying to myself, "Jim, you've looked that monster in the face and you don't have to be afraid of it anymore."

Eugene O'Neill captured the feeling of this moment in his play, *Lazarus Laughed*. The scene is a dinner party, a week or so after the raising. Lazarus's friends are all back together, this time celebrating his new-found life. Like all of us, they begin recounting their memories of the event. One of the guests describes the scene in these words:

I helped to pry away the stone so I was right beside him. I found myself kneeling, but between my fingers I watched Jesus and Lazarus. Jesus looked into his face for what seemed a long time and suddenly Lazarus said "Yes" as if he were answering a question in Jesus' eyes.

Then Jesus smiled sadly but with tenderness, as one who from a distance of years of sorrow remembers happiness. And then Lazarus knelt and kissed Jesus' feet and both of them smiled and Jesus blessed him and called him "My Brother" and went away; and Lazarus, looking after Him, began to laugh softly like a man in love with God! Such a laugh I never heard! It made my ears drunk! It was like wine! And though I was half-dead with fright I found myself laughing, too!

Later in the play, Lazarus himself recounts his resurrection:

I heard the heart of Jesus laughing in my heart . . . and my heart reborn to love of life cried "Yes!" and I laughed in the laughter of God!

The word of hope for the Christian faith is not that we will escape death. The hope is that in Christ we have victory over death. We, too, shall laugh with the laughter of God.

I had a friend in seminary who had taught high school before God called him to preach. He had two elementary-school-age sons and was serving a rural church while going to school. One day he took his boys with him for a funeral. As was the custom, they all watched as the coffin was lowered into the ground and then one by one the relatives came by to throw a handful of dirt into the grave. It's not a bad ritual. The boys watched it all, and on the way home the younger son asked, "Daddy, is that what happens when you die? They put you in a hole in the ground?" Before my friend could reply, the older son jumped in and said, "Yeah,

that's what happens. But don't worry, Jesus is strong
enough to get you out of that hole!"

Revelation brings the Bible to its grand finale with the
triumphant witness of men and women who have lived and
died by faith and now are in that white-robed throng
singing and laughing on the other side. They know by
experience what we affirm by faith: Jesus is the resurrection
and the life. Those who believe in him, even though they
die, they shall live. We do not need to be afraid of the big,
bad wolf anymore!

> O God, who gave us birth,
> you are ever more ready to hear than we are to pray.
> You know our needs before we ask, and our ignorance in
>   asking.
> Give to us now your grace,
> that as we shrink before the mystery of death
> we may see the light of eternity.
> Speak to us once more your solemn message of life and of
>   death.
> Help us to live as those who are prepared to die.
> And when our summons comes,
> may we die as those who go forth to live,
> so that living or dying, our life may be in you,
> and nothing in life or in death will be able to separate us
> from your great love in Christ Jesus our Lord. Amen.
> —*A Service of Death and Resurrection*

15

EXTRAVAGANT GRATITUDE

> Would you know who is the greatest saint in the
> world? It is not he who prays most or fasts most; it is
> not he who gives most alms, or is most eminent for
> temperance, chastity, or justice; but is is he who is
> always thankful to God, . . . who receives everything
> as an instance of God's goodness, and has a heart
> always ready to praise God for it.
> —William Law

Read Psalm 16, Luke 7:36-50

I once heard of a visiting bishop who preached in the chapel at Yale. He took as his outline the four letters, *Y, A, L, E*. He held forth for ten minutes on *Youth*. The audience was unimpressed. He went on seventeen minutes about *Ambition*. By now, the entire congregation was asleep. Undaunted, he preached four minutes on *Loyalty*, winding up with three minutes and fifteen seconds on *Energy*. At the close of the service, he followed the choir in procession down the aisle and found a student in the last row still kneeling in prayer. He leaned over and said, "Perhaps you would be good enough to tell me what I said that moved you so deeply." The young man answered, "I was just offering a prayer of thanks that I go to Yale and not the Massachusetts Institute of Technology." If you look hard enough, you can

117

always find something for which to be grateful! Gratitude is at the heart of Luke's story of Simon's houseful of Pharisees and a nameless woman who walks in off the street. The contrast between them could hardly have been stronger.

The Pharisees were the Moral Majority of their day: law-abiding, clean-living folks who knew exactly what was moral and what was not. Their major occupation was to check up on everyone else's morality. Then there was this woman. Though the story doesn't spell it out precisely, we can assume that her sin was sexual immorality. At first glance, the story appears to be a contrast of the righteous versus the unrighteous, the moral versus the immoral. That's obvious, and that was the only contrast Simon could see. But Jesus saw a deeper, far more important contrast between the woman and the Pharisees. He described it this way: "I came into your home, and you gave me no water for my feet. . . . You did not welcome me with a kiss. . . . You provided no olive oil for my head" (7:44-46, TEV). All of these were common courtesies, though they may sound strange to us. Simon hadn't even treated Jesus to the ordinary standards of hospitality.

Jesus asked, "Do you see this woman? . . . She has washed my feet with her tears and dried them with her hair. . . . She has not stopped kissing my feet since I came. . . . She has covered my feet with perfume" (7:44-46, TEV).

Jesus described the difference in the attitude behind the actions with a riddle. Two men owe money to a money-lender. One only owes a small amount, fifty coins. The other owes a fortune, five hundred coins. Neither could pay it back. In an act of unexpected generosity, the lender cancels both debts. "Who," he asked, "will be the most grateful?" Simon answered, "The one who was forgiven most." Jesus said, "You are right" (7:41-43).

The most important contrast between the woman and

the Pharisees was not in their goodness, but in their gratitude; not in the measure of their righteousness, but in the measure of their response to the generosity of God. These Pharisees thought they were getting just what they deserved; but the woman, knowing that she had received infinitely more than she could ever ask or think, responded in extravagant gratitude.

The story is told of a man who went to have his portrait painted. As he sat down in front of the artist, he said, "Be sure to do me justice." The artist responded, "You don't need justice; what you need is mercy." The truth is that if God dealt with us only with justice, if we got only what we deserved, we wouldn't like it. God is far better than that. God deals with us on the basis of generosity and grace. God gives us far more than we deserve, far more than we earn, far more than we have any right to expect. Therefore, the most appropriate response is extravagant gratitude, the kind of gratitude the writer of Psalm 16 felt when he wrote:

> All the good things I have come from you.
> ....
> You, Lord, are all I have,
>   and you give me all I need;
> ....
> How wonderful are your gifts to me;
>   how good they are!
> —vv. 2, 5-6

The story of the Pharisees and the woman cuts directly across the grain of the most common assumption upon which most of us operate. The assumption is this: everything I have is mine; I earned it, and I can do with it whatever I want. This is a half-truth and therefore also a half-lie. The half-truth is the second half. You can do what you want with what you have. Your time, your energy, your body, your mind, your relationships, your money, your

119

freedom, your opportunities—you can do with them what you want. You can use or abuse them, save or squander them. It's up to you.

That's the half-truth. The half-lie is the front end, the assumption that everything we have is ours, that we earned it, and we deserve it. Both the Bible and human experience say that is a lie. We brought nothing into this world, and we will take nothing from it. You don't find luggage racks in maternity wards and you can't hook a U-Haul to a hearse. In the meantime, everything we have is on loan to us from a gracious, generous God.

They say that Charles Darwin kept a notebook in which he used to jot down all the things that contradicted his theories. He knew that those would be precisely the things he would tend to forget. I wonder if we shouldn't keep that kind of a notebook to record all the things we have received, things we never earned or did anything to deserve, because those are precisely the things we tend to forget. Here are some things I would list in my notebook.

I was born in the United States. Put that in my notebook. I could have been born in the barren desert sands of Ethiopia, the child of starvation. I could have been born in the black ghettos of South Africa, under the demonic rule of a white minority. I could have been born in a hundred places under the oppression of Communism. But I was born in the United States. I didn't earn or deserve that. It was given to me as a gift.

I was also born into a Christian home, surrounded by people who knew the love of God and did everything in their power to help me experience that love. Put that in the notebook. I could have been born into a home where no one cared, where I had to learn to survive on my own, where the only mention of God would have been in the rampant profanity of our day. I didn't deserve or earn the home I had. It was a gift.

The New English translation of Psalm 16:6 reads: "The lines fall for me in pleasant places." And they do and have. Put that in my notebook. When I was a child growing up in Western Pennsylvania, who would have ever guessed that the lines of my life would lead through the bluegrass of Kentucky, where I met (or was I given?) my wife and some of the closest friends I've ever had? Who would have guessed that the lines would lead to Florida? I didn't ask for that; I didn't earn or deserve it. It was given to me as a gift.

To be sure, I have tried to be a responsible steward of it all. I have chosen to use rather than abuse it, to save rather than squander it, but the deepest truth is that I have been given far more than I have earned; I have received infinitely more than I deserve.

Mark Trotter, the pastor at First United Methodist Church in San Diego, tells of a psychiatrist friend who has a standard response for people who feel that life has been unfair to them. He says, "Take out the contract on life. Look at the small print. Is there anything there that says that life owes you anything?" After that, everything else is a gift.

I learned this lesson from a man I met early in my career. He was not famous or wealthy. He worked most of his life as a shoe salesman at Fountain's Clothing Store in De Land, Florida. When I arrived in Florida, he was moving into the final stages of his battle with cancer. He was in pain most of the time, unable to do very much to help himself. However, if asked how the man was doing, his son would say, "Well, it's rough, really rough. But my dad figures that when you put it all in the balance, life has been so good to him that nothing that happens from here on out could change that."

When he died, he did not leave a large estate of material goods. He did leave a son who is one of the finest Christian businessmen I've ever met. He also left on me the memory of a man who knew what the psalmist meant when he said,

All the good things I have come from you.
. . . .
You, Lord, are all I have,
   and you give me all I need;
   my future is in your hands.
How wonderful are your gifts to me;
   how good they are!
                —Psalm 16:2, 5-6, TEV

Take out your own notebook and begin your list. Perhaps you, like the grateful woman, will respond to God's extravagant goodness with extravagant gratitude.

For all that has been—Thanks!
To all that shall be—Yes!
             —Dag Hammarskjöld

16

ALL THE DIFFERENCE IN THE WORLD!

All I can say is, as one aging and singularly
unimportant fellow man, that I have conscientiously
looked far and wide, inside and outside my own
head and heart, and I have found nothing other than
this man and his words which offers any answer to
the dilemmas of this tragic, troubled time. If his
light has gone out, then, as far as I am concerned,
there is no light.

—Malcolm Muggeridge

Read Colossians 1:15-23

I have recently come to understand a new concept for me: "sensory overload." Sensory overload describes my memory of Radio City Music Hall. The great organ began to rumble, filling that cavernous building with sound that literally vibrated your seat; the orchestra rose magically out of the pit and floated to the back of the stage; the Rockettes kicked up their heels in light and dazzling color. I felt that my senses of sight and hearing were not capable of taking it all in.

Sensory overload is also what I feel every time I try to wrap my imagination around some of the words from St. Paul to the Christians in Colossae. How can my senses, my human mind and imagination, begin to take them all in?

"Christ is the visible likeness of the invisible God. . . . God created the whole universe through him and for him. . . . In union with him all things have their proper place" (1:15-17, TEV). That's sensory overload of the highest dimension. Paul spells out for us in cosmic terms the world of difference that Christ makes in our understanding of God.

How do you understand God? Who is God in your experience? Paul says that Christ is "the visible likeness of an invisible God," the tangible expression of that which we will never be able to touch, the visible expression of that which we will never be able to see.

In this verse Paul uses the fascinating little Greek word, *eikōn*. Literally translated it comes very close to our word *portrait*. It is like the photograph on your driver's license or your passport. When a contract was being signed, the *eikōn* would be included as a description of the identifying characteristics of the parties in the contract. Paul is saying that it is as though the eternal God has signed a contract with this universe and has included a self-portrait, some identifying characteristics, the *eikōn*. That portrait is nothing more or less than the life, the words, the work, and the spirit of Jesus of Nazareth. If you ask me what God is like, I would say to you, "Here are the identifying characteristics." This is as much of God as I can conceive or understand. "Christ is the visible likeness of the invisible God."

It makes a world of difference in our understanding of God if we begin by saying, "God is like Jesus." I can see that, touch it, hear it, know it in human history. We have a portrait of God in Jesus of Nazareth.

Paul goes on to affirm that Christ makes a world of difference in how we understand the universe around us, the world in which we live. "Through [Christ] God created everything in heaven and on earth, the seen and the unseen things. . . . God created the whole universe through him and for him. Christ existed before all things, and in union with him all things have their proper place" (1:16-17, TEV). It makes a gigantic difference how we understand the world in which we live if we believe that it was all created for, through, and in Jesus Christ, and that in Christ it all holds together.

The modern, technical world in which we live has very specific instructions for everything. Attached to any piece of electrical equipment, whether a kitchen appliance, a stereo or television, or anything else, are clear instructions on how it works and how its owner must operate it. When you buy a piece of equipment like this, you will often open the box to find an important notice in large type so you can't miss it. It will say something like: "Notice: This equipment is intended to operate on AC current only. Operation of this equipment on any other current may cause serious damage to delicate internal parts. If this equipment is operated on any other current, the manufacturer's guarantee no longer applies."

Paul is saying something like that about our world. This world is meant to operate in the way revealed in the words, the life, and the witness of Jesus Christ. If you try to run this universe on any other current, you may risk serious damage to some of its parts. If you try to run this world in any other way than the way revealed in Christ, the manufacturer's guarantee may no longer apply.

As I look at our world, I would say that human history is proving Paul to be correct. We have tried to run this world on selfishness, greed, and arrogance. Someday may God help us to discover that the way revealed in Jesus Christ is the way that the world was meant to be run.

E. Stanley Jones knew the realities of the twentieth century. He experienced life on nearly every continent, listened and dialogued with men and women of many races, religions, and cultures. His experience led him to the conclusion that the way of Christ is written into the fabric of human

125

life. "There is a way stamped into everything—it is the way life is made to work; and that way is the Christian way." He compared the way of Christ to the musical note A 440, which is the standard to which all musical instruments in an orchestra are tuned. "Everything that departs from that note is discord, and hence torture. . . . In Jesus the standard note of human living is struck. Everything that tunes to that note catches the music of the spheres; everything that departs from it is discord and torture." The twentieth century is proving Jones to be correct. We will either learn to live by the way revealed in Christ or we will destroy ourselves in greed and selfish abandon. The universe was made for Christ and by Christ and it is in Christ that there is hope of holding it together.

Paul tightens the focus on the way the world is intended to live when he writes, "Through Christ God chose to reconcile the whole universe to himself, making peace through the shedding of his blood upon the cross" (1:20, NEB). The gravitational center of all creation is nothing more or less than the sacrificial love of God revealed in Jesus Christ. The center of human life is not power, might, greed, arrogance, or selfishness. At the center of human life and history is the cross. God intends for life to be lived on the basis of sacrificial, self-giving love.

Finally, Paul brings us down to a profoundly personal corner of our lives. It makes a world of difference to know the living Christ in our own experience. "God's plan is to make known his secret to his people, this rich and glorious secret which he has for all people. And the secret is that Christ is in you, which means that you will share in the glory of God" (1:27, TEV). Later on in the letter, he reiterates this idea when he tells these Colossian Christians, "You have been raised to life with Christ, so set your hearts on the things that are in heaven. . . . Your real life is Christ" (3:1, 4, TEV).

The amazing affirmation of the gospel is that this cosmic Christ, this Christ who is the visible expression of the invisible God, this Christ who is at the heart of all creation, comes to live in your life and in mine.

When I was in college, I ran into a campus movement that boiled the whole Christian faith down to "Four Spiritual Laws." It seemed overly simplistic to me. I am still not sure you can put the whole Christian gospel into four little sentences, but they had, complete with charts to go with them. One of those charts had a large circle that represented a person's life. Inside that circle were family, friends, work, career, and, at the center, a large chair, a throne. These people would show you the chart and ask, "Who sits on the throne in your life?"

It may have been simplistic, but it was the right question. This is the question the gospel continually holds in front of us. Who sits on the throne in your life? Who has the preeminent position in your experience? Who sets your values, your direction? Who shapes the attitudes, the desires by which you live? The affirmation of the gospel is that Christ is meant to be king, to sit on the throne of your life and mine. The tangled web of life begins to unravel when we experience Christ as our king, our Lord, our master. The secret is this: Christ in you, the hope of glorious things to come.

We experience Christ in us in a variety of ways. Let me share one witness that speaks powerfully to me. Frederick Buechner was twenty-seven years old, living in New York City, trying unsuccessfully to fall in love and to write a novel. One day, for reasons he could never quite explain, he decided to go hear a famous preacher. Though he doesn't tell it in the following narrative, in his autobiography we find out that the famous preacher was George Buttrick and the church was Madison Avenue Presbyterian Church in New York City. It was about the time that Queen Elizabeth

II was crowned in Great Britain. He says that the preacher was playing variations on the theme of coronation, picking up on Queen Elizabeth's coronation in Westminster Abbey.

> All I remember of what he said is the very last, and that not well, just one phrase of it, in fact, that I'm sure of. He said that Jesus Christ refused a crown when Satan offered it in the wilderness, or something like that. He said that the kingdom of Jesus was not of this world. And yet again and again, he said, Jesus was crowned in the hearts of those who believed in him, crowned as king. I remember thinking that was a nice enough image, as images in sermons go, and I remember how the preacher looked up there in the pulpit twitching around a good deal, it seemed to me, and plucking at the lapels of his black gown. And then he went on just a few sentences more.
>
> He said that unlike Elizabeth's coronation in the Abbey, this coronation of Jesus in the believer's heart took place among confession—and I thought, yes, yes, confession—and tears, he said—and I thought tears, yes, perfectly plausible that the coronation of Jesus in the believing heart should take place among confession and tears. And then with his head bobbing up and down so that his glasses glittered, he said in his odd, sandy voice, the voice of an old nurse, that the coronation of Jesus took place among confession and tears and then, as God was and is my witness, great laughter, he said. Jesus is crowned among confession and tears and great laughter, and at the phrase *great laughter*, for reasons that I have never satisfactorily understood, the great wall of China crumbled and Atlantis rose up out of the sea, and on Madison Avenue, at 73rd Street, tears leapt from my eyes as though I had been struck across the face.

I cannot predict how it will happen for you. It may or may not have the emotion Buechner felt. But I want to ask you, has Christ been crowned in your life? Among confession, yes, perhaps with tears, yes, and with great laughter?

He is the visible expression of the invisible God. He is the

one who is at the center of creation. But the best news of all
is that he is also Christ in you, bringing with him the hope of
glorious things to come.

> Thou who art over us,
> Thou who art one of us,
> Thou who *art*—
> Also within us,
> May all see Thee—in me also,
> May I prepare the way for Thee,
> May I thank Thee for all that shall fall to my lot,
> May I also not forget the needs of others,
> Keep me in Thy love
> As Thou wouldest that all should be kept in mine.
> May everything in this my being be directed to Thy glory
> And may I never despair.
> For I am under Thy hand,
> And in Thee is all power and goodness.
>
> Give me a pure heart—that I may see Thee,
> A humble heart—that I may hear Thee,
> A heart of love—that I may serve Thee,
> A heart of faith—that I may abide in Thee.
>
> —Dag Hammarskjöld

Questions ─────────

for Thought and Discussion

Chapter 1
1. What does it mean for you to "put yourself completely under the influence of Jesus"? To what can you compare this in your own life?
2. Which of the "snapshots" from Matthew speak most directly to your life? How do you identify with any of these characters?
3. What changes would be necessary in the daily pattern of your life for you to "learn Christ," "think Christ," and "live Christ"?
4. Discuss your willingness to experiment for one week with the question, "What would Jesus do?"

Chapter 2
1. How does Matthew 6:25-31 speak to you?
2. What gives value or worth to your life? Do you find your personal identity in your work? Your accomplishments? God's love? Discuss your sources of value.
3. Whom have you known like the businessman described here? How were they the same?
4. What does "conversion" mean to you? How did you respond to the description of "confession"? "Repentance"? "Trust"? How would you apply them to your own life?

Chapter 3
1. Have you ever faced an experience similar to the loss of

the stillborn child described here? Share that experience with your group.
2. What does it mean for you to know that Jesus experienced "the feeling of our infirmities"?
3. Have you ever pictured God as *The Thinker*? Why?
4. Can you identify with Jesus in the Garden of Gethsemane? How?
5. Have you seen suffering transformed into strength? When and where?

Chapter 4

1. How would you have answered the letter with which the chapter opens?
2. Look again at the man beside the pool. How do you suppose he felt when Jesus asked, "Do you want to be healed?"
3. Do you have a "thorn in the flesh"? How have you dealt with it?
4. Do you believe that "God's primary intention is always for wholeness"? How is this belief manifested?
5. What examples have you seen of the way God is "working still"?
6. What does it mean for you to hear God say, "My grace is sufficient for you"?

Chapter 5

1. When did you last have the blues?
2. Have you ever felt that Jesus was walking with you as he did with the men on the Emmaus Road? How did this feel?
3. Do you believe that "only those who . . . mourn their loss . . . have any hope of being comforted"? Why?
4. How would you define or describe *hope*?
5. If available, read the poem "Renascence" by Edna St. Vincent Millay.

Chapter 6

1. Have you ever been afraid? Describe that experience to your group.
2. Have you ever thought of fear as a positive force? When?

3. Look again at the three principles outlined here. How have you experienced this process in your own life?
4. How have you seen fear transformed into creative action?

Chapter 7

1. Have you ever felt like a porcupine in your relationships with others? Why?
2. In our own time, what does it mean to judge people by human standards?
3. What difference would it make for you to see people as persons for whom Jesus Christ died?
4. Have you ever had someone see hidden possibilities in you that no one else recognized? How did that feel? Have you done that for someone else?
5. Can you see yourself as God's agent of reconciliation? What persons have fulfilled that role in your life? How did they do it?

Chapter 8

1. "Most of us . . . have inherited a picnic basket full of bigotry, fears, and intolerance." What are some of yours?
2. Read the story of the Good Samaritan. With whom do you identify in that story? Explain why.
3. How do you respond, on an emotional level, to the story of the child named Fine?
4. What practical difference does Jesus make in your relationships with people who are radically different than you?

Chapter 9

1. Share your most recent "wilderness experience" with your group. How did temptation come to you?
2. Of the specific temptations of Jesus, which is the closest to your own experience?
3. What would it mean for you to overcome evil with good? Do you think this is a practical possibility in our world? Have you seen it happen?
4. How have you experienced "negative goodness" or "positive goodness"?
5. Read Romans 12. How does it speak to your life?

Chapter 10

1. Share your own experience with loneliness. How has it touched you?
1. How would you have felt if you had been with Jesus for that Passover celebration? How must Jesus have felt?
3. How have you experienced "the transforming friendship"? What have you done to nurture that kind of relationship with Jesus?
4. "Everyone who belongs to Christ belongs to everyone who belongs to Christ." How do you respond to that statement?
5. What practical steps could you take to become a builder of bridges?

Chapter 11

1. Have you ever felt like a grasshopper? What was the situation?
2. Can you understand why the people of Israel accepted the majority report? Are optimists like Caleb always in the minority? Why?
3. Can you identify with the disciples in the story of the feeding of the multitude? When have you felt that way? What resources do you have that could be offered to Christ to "feed the multitude"?
4. Have you known people like Alyce? Share their story with your group.
5. What specific situations do you now face that require an attitude like that of Caleb? Share that situation with the group and ask them to pray for you in it.

Chapter 12

1. This chapter tells the stories of individuals whose lives made a difference in their world. Can you add personal stories to the list? Who do you know who has made a difference? What did they do?
2. Have you ever doubted the influence one person can have in our world? Discuss why.
3. As you look at the present world, what issues raise the deepest concern for you?
4. What are some specific ways God is calling you to be an

influence for goodness? What are the specific gifts God
has given you to use?

Chapter 13

1. When did you last experience "soul drain"? How did you
   cope with it?
2. Do you accept the idea that there is healing power in a
   reaffirmation of mystery? Look again at the Killinger
   quote. How does it speak to you?
3. How is your spiritual discipline? Have you felt its
   influence on your life? What can you do to develop
   meaningful patterns of discipline for your life?
4. Again we return to the "ministry of friendship." Have you
   noticed how often this theme emerges? Could it be that
   most of the difference Jesus makes in our lives comes
   through other people? Explain why.
5. Read Ephesians 3:14-19 in several translations. How
   would it change your life if this prayer became a reality
   for you?

Chapter 14

1. Share you earliest memory of death. How have your
   feelings changed across the years?
2. Did you feel the surprise in the story of Lazarus? Is it the
   kind of surprise that would make you laugh? Why?
3. Read the passage from *Lazarus Laughed* aloud. How does it
   make you feel?
4. Does the assurance that "Jesus is strong enough to get
   you out of that hole" help you break the fear of death?
5. Read First Corinthians 15 as an act of affirmation.

Chapter 15

1. Would you agree that gratitude is at the heart of the
   difference between the Pharisees and the woman in this
   story from Luke?
2. Have you ever assumed that "Everything I have is mine; I
   earned it, and I can do with it whatever I want"? How
   has this chapter caused you to question that assumption?
3. What are some of the things you would list in your
   notebook as things you have received and for which you
   need to be grateful?

4. Who are the people you have known who have lived with a sense of extravagant gratitude? How could you see this in their lives?
5. Read Psalm 16 aloud and close your time together in prayer.

Chapter 16

1. How have you experienced sensory overload? Do you experience it from this passage of scripture?
2. What does it mean for you to say "God is like Jesus"?
3. What difference does it make for you to believe that God created everything in, through, and for Christ?
4. What difference would it make for you to allow Jesus to "sit on the throne" of your life? Are you willing to do it?
5. Share what this study has meant to you and how you plan to apply your discoveries to your own life. You may share your response with the author by writing in care of the publishers.

Acknowledgments

137

James A. Harnish is the pastor of St. Luke's United Methodist Church at Windermere in Orlando, Florida, a congregation he helped to organize in 1979. He and his wife Marsha have two daughters, Carrie Lynn and Deborah Jeanne.

Mr. Harnish has served other United Methodist congregations in Florida. He has also written *What Will You Do with King Jesus?*, published by The Upper Room.